VOICES OF NEGRITUDE

VOICES OF NÉGRITUDE

EDWARD A. JONES

THE EXPRESSION OF BLACK EXPERIENCE IN THE POETRY OF SENGHOR CÉSAIRE & DAMAS

JUDSON PRESS, Valley Forge

VOICES OF NÉGRITUDE

The English translations in this book have been compiled from different sources by the author. The sources of each of these translations are indicated. The translations for which there are no sources listed are those by the author.

International Standard Book No. 0-8170-0529-3
Library of Congress Catalog Card No. 75-152062

Printed in the U.S.A.

To my wife, Virginia Lacy Jones

Contents

Preface

The fortunes of *Négritude* since it was a subject of café table disputation in the Paris of the thirties have indeed been remarkable. For the sensitivities of the young Damas, Césaire, and Senghor, the contemplation of an academic and intellectual tradition which accepted unquestioningly the image of the black man as an unthinking primitive was a searing experience. Their determination to modify that view both for themselves and for others was based in part on their awareness of the extraordinary vitality demonstrated by blacks in the United States during the Harlem Renaissance of the twenties. The names of such men as DuBois, Locke, Woodson, and James Weldon Johnson were well known to the Paris group. Secondly, they had knowledge of the intellectual vigor and ferment of black Haiti as exemplified in the work of Georges Sylvain, Dantès Bellegarde, and Jean Price-Mars.

They were also indebted to the publications of two European pioneers of African studies, the German Frobenius and the Frenchman Delafosse, whose positive though somewhat quaint perspectives on traditional African societies provided a counterpoise to the typical European view of the black man which had prevailed since the Enlightenment, a curious term to describe an epoch during which the transatlantic slave trade flourished so mightily.

Négritude grew out of the encounter of the sons of Mother Africa and the children of her diaspora from the Antilles, South America, and North America. This encounter produced the sense of a common destiny. From it came the formulation of pride in blackness based on a sense of a shared cultural inheritance.

A little-known chapter in the development of *Négritude* is the catalytic participation of black Americans who were present in Paris in the thirties as a part of the student population. Among these Mercer Cook and Edward A. Jones were of great importance. They provided a link to the lives and personalities of black American intellectuals and artists such as Langston Hughes and Sterling Brown. The triumvirate of *Négritude* owes them a freely acknowledged debt for a major component of its work. It is especially appropriate, then, that Professor Jones, who has taught and lectured for many years at Morehouse and Atlanta University on the major figures of *Négritude,* should share his view of them with a larger public.

RICHARD A. LONG
Atlanta University

VOICES OF NÉGRITUDE

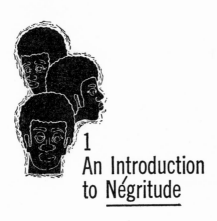

1
An Introduction
to <u>Négritude</u>

In the United States, the black-consciousness movement in its activist form is a child of the 1960's. It was brought to the attention of the general public by the black student protests and sit-ins of the first several years of that decade. The movement was the logical outcome of years of oppression and discrimination imposed by a racist society, and it was the culmination of less spectacular resistance and less fruitful sporadic protests that go back to slavery and the Underground Railroad.

The success of the revolt of blacks in Montgomery, Alabama, against Jim-Crow bus laws, a southwide practice that was patently unjust and deeply humiliating, under the capable and inspired leadership of the late Dr. Martin Luther King, Jr., in 1958, encouraged young, impatient, and idealistic black students to make an all-out attack on all forms of segregation in the South. The outcome of their nonviolent efforts, despite the use of fire hoses, police dogs, frequent jailings, intimidation, and other forms of violence to maintain the status quo, is too well known for detailed consideration here.

Black awareness in the United States as a concept and as a literary phenomenon may be traced back to such black intellectuals as Dr. W. E. B. DuBois, whose *Souls of Black Folk* had become the bible of the black militants before Frantz Fanon's writings, and the earliest Afro-American writers; and it reached its apogee during the so-called Negro Renaissance of the 1920's, with Claude McKay, Countee Cullen, Langston Hughes, Jean Toomer, Sterling Brown *et al.,* who played important roles in the birth of black awareness among students and writers of African origin who were enrolled as students in Paris in the late 1920's and in the 1930's. The students in question were from French Africa, the French West Indies (Martinique, Guadeloupe, and Haiti), and French Guiana in South America.

The principal architects of the concept and the term *Négritude* were Aimé Césaire, of Martinique, French West Indies; Léopold Sédar Senghor, of Senegal, West Africa (now its president); and Léon Damas, of Guadeloupe, French West Indies.

Césaire, Damas, and Senghor were among a group of black students in Paris who, in the late twenties and early thirties, became aware of their common heritage and their cultural isolation in an ambience which, though not hostile, was either indifferent to them or expected them to be black Frenchmen, renouncing thus their African background and blending perfectly with their Parisian cultural, though obviously not with their ethnical, environment. In dress, speech, and manners, they were expected to reflect the culture and customs of the French. Their education was French. History was taught them with a French bias, which, of course, meant that colonialism was viewed as a blessing and not a bane to blacks "fortunate" enough to have the French for colonial masters. African and West Indian blacks under French rule were expected to develop into what some years later Frantz Fanon was to characterize as *Black Skin, White Masks.* Although a handful of select blacks were fortunate enough to study in Paris, the intellectual Mecca of the West, the wretched masses of their people back home were victims of poverty, ignorance, and disease largely because of colonial exploitation, discrimination, insults, and humiliation. These were conditions from which they, as expatriates ostensibly accepted by the French, could not escape, even if they had wanted to do so. It was the realization of this unhappy situation which brought these Afro-French blacks together in organized efforts to assess their plight and to take some sort of action to remedy it. They were intellectuals, and as such their activism was to be of

14

an intellectual order. They founded two papers, the short-lived *L'Étudiant Noir,* around 1932, and later *Légitime Défense,* to serve as organs of black student thinking and protest in Paris — to assert the black personality and to defend African social and cultural values. In this, they made *cause commune* (common cause) with a few Negro Americans who were also students in Paris at that time and who joined them in meetings at the *salon littéraire* (literary gathering place) of an interested, sympathetic Parisian, Mlle. Andrée Nardal, where topics of common interest and works of Afro-American writers were discussed. The concept of *Négritude* thus came into being, born of that association and those discussions. The term *Négritude* first appeared in print in an article published by Aimé Césaire in *Légitime Défense,* but it did not gain widespread recognition until the publication of Césaire's first poetic collection, *Cahier d'un retour au pays natal* which was written in 1937-1938 but was published only in 1947 by Bordas after having appeared in *Présence Africaine,* an excellent and scholarly black magazine that was also a product of black intellectualism and that appeared simultaneously in Dakar, Senegal, and in Paris. Moreover, René Maran's Goncourt Prize-winning novel of protest, *Batoula* (1921), exercised a great impact on the *élan* toward the black solidarity out of which the concept of *Négritude* was to emerge. Thus was awakened the conscience of young French-speaking Africans and West Indians (including Haitians), who grouped themselves under the leadership of Senghor, Césaire, and Damas with the able assistance of the eminent Haitian intellectual and senior statesman, Dr. Jean Price-Mars.

The use of the term *Négritude* in *Cahier,* whose full title is translated as *Notebook of a Return to the Native Country,* occurs when Césaire tells of an experience in Paris which was a turning point in his way of thinking about his blackness, his *Négritude,* if you will.

Césaire was on a Paris streetcar one evening when a homely, ridiculously dressed Negro was seated facing him. This hapless black, an obvious misfit in this urbane setting, became instantly the object of derision on the part of other (white) passengers. His clothes were too big for him, and in every way he "swore with" his surroundings, as the French say, "His nose," Césaire says, "seemed a peninsula adrift, his very *Négritude* paled under the action of a tireless tawing" (*"Son nez,"* Césaire says, *"qui semblait une péninsule en dérade et sa négritude même qui se décolorait sous l'action d'une inlassable mégie"*).[1]

Further described, the Negro who was the subject of general derision was, according to Césaire, "as big as a pongo" but he tried to make himself small on that dirty tramway bench . . . and to "relax [hide] his gigantic legs and his trembling hungry pug's fists," an ungainly Negro without rhythm or measure, "a Negro whose eyes were bloodshot, weary." "Poverty, undeniably, had worked on him no end," leaving him unshaven, arched of back, panic-stricken — in a word, a hideous, ill-tempered, melancholy Negro: "a comical, ugly Negro, and the women behind me laughed as they looked at him." [2]

Admittedly, a victim of cowardice, Césaire tells us that he turned his eyes away, proclaiming, "I had nothing in common with that monkey." The ultimate effect on the poet was, however, this: It served to make him reexamine his position as a black man in a white culture, to reassess his whole racial philosophy and outlook. The result was that he came to realize that his fate and that of the ridiculous black on the Paris tramway were inextricably linked to one another — that, in spite of his French exterior, he was also a black and basically no different from the humblest, most ignorant, most ridiculous black. This realization was a turning point in his life and led Césaire to declare, as if in a profession of religious faith, "I accept, I accept all that . . . [all that *Négritude*]" (*"j'accepte, j'accepte tout cela* . . . [*toute cette négritude*]"*).[3]

Since the publication of *Cahier*, the term *Négritude* has been widely used and variously defined, connoting different things to different people; but it has remained largely an esoteric term, used and understood by a relatively limited segment of humanity: those interested in Afro-French writers from 1930 to the present, especially the protest writers, Senghor, Césaire, Damas *et al.*, who,

[1] Aimé Césaire, *Cahier d'un retour au pays natal* [Return to my native land], tr. Emile Snyder (Paris: Présence Africaine, 1956), pp. 100, 101, 103.
[2] *Ibid.*, pp. 100, 102, 104.
[3] *Ibid.*, pp. 136, 137.

unlike the white proletariat, use poetry as their literary medium. These writers are not second-rate rhymesters but top-flight artisans of the medium, men who have mastered all the tools of the trade and who are recognized even in France as worthy of the highest plaudits in the most difficult of literary genres, one of them, Léopold Senghor, having been awarded the International Poetry Prize in 1963.

Senghor gave us the best definition of *Négritude,* which he characterizes as "the cultural patrimony, the values, and especially the spirit of black-African civilization" *("le patrimoine culturel, les valeurs et surtout l'esprit de la civilisation Négro-Africaine").* Elsewhere, he calls it "the sum-total of black values and civilizations" *("l'ensemble des valeurs et des civilisations noires").*[4]

As we assess the use of the concept and the term *Négritude* in the works of the writers under consideration here, we are inclined to define it, in a larger context which includes the above definitions, as the totality of the black experience, including all the poverty, suffering, humiliation, and injustices which have gone into it.

Each of the men previously characterized as architects of the concept and term *Négritude* expresses his *Négritude* and his reaction to it in accordance with his personal experiences and his philosophy of human and interracial relations. Senghor, at once the most eloquent and the most restrained spokesman for *Négritude,* will be discussed first.

[4] Léopold Sédar Senghor, *Entretien de Juin,* as quoted in Lilyan Kesteloot, *Ecrivains noirs de la langue française* (Brussels, Belgium: Institut de Sociologie, Université de Bruxelles, 1963) , p. 110.

2
Léopold Sédar Senghor

Senghor was born in 1906, of rather well-to-do parents, in the Senegalese town of Joal, which he immortalizes in a poem, *"A Joal,"* of his first collection, entitled *Chants d'ombre* [Songs of Darkness]. He did his elementary studies *(études primaires)* at Ngasobie and Dakar, the latter city being the modern and attractive capital of his native Senegal. He belongs to the Sérère tribe. Young Senghor was sent to Paris for his secondary and higher education, the former having been done at the Lycée Louis-le-Grand, an old and prestigious school that boasts such distinguished graduates as the seventeenth-century playwright Molière and France's current president, Georges Pompidou, a contemporary and friend of Senghor (one of his poems is dedicated to M. Pompidou); and the latter having been obtained at the Sorbonne and the École normale supérieure, France's highest teacher-training institution that admits only the intellectual, the very choicest *(crème de la crème)*. He came out of the École normale supérieure as *agrégé de grammaire*, a highly competitive degree of scholastic achievement, with a specialization in French grammar, required of candidates for positions as teachers in the French *lycées*. In 1935, Senghor was appointed a professor in the Lycée of Tours, France, being the first African to teach in a French secondary school *(lycée)*. He

19

studied African languages, which he later taught in École des hautes études coloniales in Paris.

In 1939, as a French subject, Senghor served in the French army and was taken prisoner by the Germans and placed in a concentration camp, from which he managed to escape. One of his poems, "Camp 1940," was inspired by his experiences in the concentration camp. When the war was over, Senghor was elected *député* from Senegal to the National Constituent Assembly *(L'Assemblée nationale constituante),* which drew up the Constitution for the Fourth Republic in France, which lasted from 1946 to 1958. In the Assembly, Senghor was appointed chairman of the committee charged with the responsibility of seeing that the new Constitution was drawn up in impeccable French — a tribute to his command of the language and a recognition of his authority as an *agrégé de grammaire.* Senghor's political philosophy and orientation lined him up with the French Socialist Party in the Assembly. He was later to write a treatise *On African Socialism,* published about 1964 and translated into English by Howard University professor and former U.S. Ambassador to Niger and Senegal, Mercer Cook.

In 1946, Senghor founded a magazine called *Condition Humaine;* and in 1947, he became editor of *Présence Africaine,* a scholarly review dedicated to black African letters and cultures. In 1948, he founded the Senegalese political party known as *le Bloc Démocratique Sénégalais* and left the French Socialist Party. In 1951, he became head of the faction of the *Indépendants d'Outremer* (Overseas Independents) in the French Chamber of Deputies, the lower legislative House under the Fourth Republic. In 1956, he was elected mayor of the Senegalese city of Thiès; and in 1958, he founded the *Bloc Sénégalais Progressiste* (Progressive Senegalese Bloc). The following year, 1959, he became President of the Federal Assembly of Mali, the former French Sudan.

The year 1960 saw a shower of national independencies fall on Africa, liberating a score of former European colonies. Senegal was among them. In August, 1960, Léopold Sédar Senghor was elected the first President of the Republic of Senegal, and today, after ten years, he still serves as the chief executive of his beloved fatherland. It is ironic that the former official residence of the governor general of French West Africa, a stately mansion overlooking the Dakar waterfront, now serves as the official residence of the president of the Republic of Senegal and is occupied by a black man who dwarfs all previous occupants in intellectual, literary, and political stature. (All of colonial French West Africa was administered from Dakar.)

The distinguished scholar, who is at once poet, president, and politician, has published the following collections of poetry: *Chants d'ombre, Hosties Noires, Éthiopiques,* and *Nocturnes,* the latter having singled him out for the *Prix International de Poésie* in 1963. M. Senghor has to his credit, also, an impressive number of prose works and articles.

After vivid childhood reminiscences in *"A Joal"* and *"Nuits de Sine"* in *Chants d'ombre,* which bring to mind DuBellay's nostalgia and regrets in *"Les Regrets,"* Senghor approaches subject matter more directly related to *Négritude.* The poem which serves best to reveal this pride in race, this tribute to blackness, is his eminently beautiful *"Femme Noire,"* which by his own admission was inspired by Claude McKay. In a celebrated passage written in 1950 on Negro-American poetry, Senghor says:

> But [Claude] McKay's lesson has finally been heard. More than the acceptance of a fact, there is developing among today's poets a faith in their race. They are convinced that it carries, along with new values, a springtime sap that will make American civilization flower again. And they have a very special cult, made up of respect and love, desire, and admiration, for the black woman, who symbolizes *Négritude.* For woman is, more than man, sensitive to the mysterious currents of life and the cosmos, more permeable to joy and sorrow. I could have you listen to "Song for the Black Virgin," by Hughes, who like a few others, writes as well in English as in [Negro] dialect.[1]

Distance, since Senghor was in France, led the poet to idealize his country and the black woman, who, to him, symbolizes it; and he makes of her the object of an imaginary crystallization in *"Femme Noire"*:

[1] Translated from Léopold Sédar Senghor, "La Poésie Negro-Américaine," *Liberté* 1, p. 117.

Femme Noire [2]

Femme nue, femme noire

Vêtue de ta couleur qui est vie, de ta forme qui est
beauté!

J'ai grandi à ton ombre; la douceur de tes mains bandait
mes yeux.

Et voilà qu'au coeur de l'Eté et de Midi, je te découvre,
Terre promise, du haut d'un haut col calciné,

Et ta beauté me foudroie en plein coeur, comme l'éclair
d'un aigle.

Femme nue, femme obscure,

Fruit mûr à la chair ferme, sombres extases du vin noir,
bouche qui fais lyrique ma bouche;

Savane aux horizons purs, savane qui frémis aux caresses
ferventes du Vent d'Est,

Tamtam sculpté, tamtam tendu qui grondes sous les
doigts du Vainqueur,

Ta voix grave de contre-alto est le chant spirituel de
l'Aimée.

Femme nue, femme obscure,

Huile que ne ride nul souffle, huile calme aux flancs
de l'athlète, aux flances des princes du Mali;

Gazelle aux attaches célestes, les perles sont étoiles sur
la nuit de ta peau,

Délices des jeux de l'Esprit, les reflets de l'or rouge sur
ta peau qui se moire;

A l'ombre de ta chevelure, s'éclaire mon angoisse aux
soleils prochains de tes yeux.

Femme nue, femme noire,

Je chante ta beauté qui passe, Forme que je fixe dans
l'Éternel,

Avant que le Destin jaloux ne te réduise en cendres pour
nourrir les racines de la Vie.

[2] Léopold Sédar Senghor, "Femme Noire," *Chants d'ombre* (Paris:
Editions du Seuil, 1945), pp. 19-20.

Black Woman [3]

Naked woman, black woman
Clothed with your colour which is life, with your form
    which is beauty!
In your shadow I have grown up; the gentleness of your
    hands was laid over my eyes.
And now, high up on the sun-baked pass, at the heart
    of summer, at the heart of noon, I come upon you,
    my Promised Land,
And your beauty strikes me to the heart like the flash
    of an eagle.

Naked woman, dark woman
Firm-fleshed ripe fruit, sombre raptures of black wine,
    mouth making lyrical my mouth
Savannah stretching to clear horizons, savannah shudder-
    ing beneath the East Wind's eager caresses
Carved tom-tom, taut tom-tom, muttering under the
    Conqueror's fingers
Your solemn contralto voice is the spiritual song of the
    Beloved.

Naked woman, dark woman
Oil that no breath ruffles, calm oil on the athlete's flanks,
    on the flanks of the Princes of Mali
Gazelle limbed in Paradise, pearls are stars on the night
    of your skin
Delights of the mind, the glinting of red gold against
    your watered skin
Under the shadow of your hair, my care is lightened by
    the neighbouring suns of your eyes.

Naked woman, black woman,
I sing your beauty that passes, the form that I fix in the
    Eternal,
Before jealous Fate turn you to ashes to feed the roots
    of life.

[3] From *Selected Poems* by Léopold Sédar Senghor. Trans-
lated and Introduced by John Reed and Clive Wake, p. 6. Copy-
right © Oxford University Press 1964. Reprinted by permission
of Atheneum Publishers, New York.

"Femme Noire" is the dream of an expatriate who wishes to immortalize the black woman as a generic concept which he wants to fix for eternity *(dans l'éternel)* before she disappears through death and/or racial mixture *(métissage).* In reply to critics who saw in the poem an element of racism, among whom was Jean-Paul Sartre, whose preface *Orphée Noir* to Senghor's *Anthologie de lo nouvelle poèsie nègre et Malgache* (1948) has become as famous as the book, Senghor replied that the glorification of womanhood has characterized writers since time immemorial. Indeed, the need to extol such values has, he said, characterized English literature from Spencer and Shakespeare to William Butler Yeats, and in France, from Marie de France to Paul Eluard.[4] Throughout the history of European letters, the Western poet has glorified the white woman because of her whiteness, as witnessed by Dante's Beatrice and Petrarch's Laura. For these bards, whiteness in womanhood represents life, love, and the ideal of beauty. This is not racism since the poet is not thinking here of racist terms.

In *"Femme Noire,"* Senghor, as a black poet, seeks to reevaluate everything that comes from black Africa: woman, art, and cultural values. It is as much a glorification of black values as it is a tribute to black womanhood.

In *Hosties Noires,* Senghor enters a second phase in his poetic career. He passes from personal poetry to collective poetry, from lyrical and nostalgic verse to nationalistic verse placed in political service. It is the period of his protest poetry, of his activist writings. He seeks identity with the lowly and the disinherited.

In later collections, such as *Nocturnes,* Senghor returns to his original muse and to contemplative poetry.

Senghor is the prototype and the spokesman *(porte-parole)* of the new French-speaking nations of black Africa, and his slogan is to assimilate French culture without being assimilated to it *(assimiler, non être assimilés).* This principle of cultural grafting, which seeks to preserve native African cultural values while adopting what is beneficial and adaptable from French culture, has produced a new Afro-French humanism that can best be

---

[4] Cf. S. Okechukwu Mezu, *Léopold Sédar Senghor el la défense et illustration de la civilisation noire* (Paris: Librairie M. Didier, 1968), p. 72.

studied in Senghor's poetry, which sings of the pride of being black with remarkably melodic and rhythmic beauty and with a deep serenity free of bitterness and vindictiveness. His song is the saga of his beloved Africa, of the Africa of the past, with its folkways and traditions; of the Africa of the present, with its hurts, its hopes, and its aspirations; of the Africa of the future, with its dreams of universal brotherhood, for which the poet longs and for which he labors assiduously. Senghor, as has been stated, is one with the simplest and lowliest peasant, and he sings of his future liberation from present-day serfdom. He, being the intellectual and states-man that he is, has to make *cause commune* with all who toil, realizing that their fate is his and his theirs.

To the great Senegalese poet-politician, Africa is the beloved country, the fatherland of unmatched and mysterious beauty. In lines of exceedingly rare poetic excellence, he succeeds in evoking the secret and mystic soul of the Dark Continent:

> Les tamtams, dans les plaines noyées, rythment ton chant,
> et ton vers est la respiration de la nuit
> et de la mer lointaine.

> The tom-toms, in the drowned plains, echo thy song,
> and thy verse is the respiration of the night
> and of the distant sea.

Referring to the white race as "the haughty one of the fortunate, or happy, races" *("la superbe des races heureuses"),* Senghor, with the characteristic patience and prudence of his people, and with true Christian toler-ance (he is a practicing Catholic), conceals any bitter-ness he might have felt for Europe and its people. There-fore, his ideas on colonial Africa, unlike those of his friend Césaire in the colonial West Indies, are devoid of hatred and resentment as they find expression in his verse. As for France, if poet Senghor harbors any animus for the former oppressors and exploiters of his Fathers, through whom he addresses France, he tactfully subdues it; and his appeal to his revered ancestors is couched in Christian charity and goodwill as regards "the lords of gold and the suburbs" *("les seigneurs de l'or et des banlieus"),* the phrase he uses to designate Europeans. Senghor sees the hand of God in the defeat of France

---

[5] Senghor, "Lettre à un poète," *Chants d'ombre,* p. 12.

in 1940, as he asserts that his own participation in that war was the occasion of a "replanting of fidelity" to France. The poet has not allowed his heart to become hardened by hate, and his dream of human brotherhood fills him with hope.

There is melancholy in Senghor's song. But there is also a powerful certainty of the vitality of his native Africa and of its mission to the world. Though keenly aware of the *oneness* of humanity and of the urgent necessity for world brotherhood, Senghor is at the same time a proud African who has not the slightest intention of renouncing his personality as an African. Yet he is a Francophile and a humanist whose admiration for French culture and whose deep human insights provide him with a broad perspective through which to view and appraise the human scene. As an African, he is convinced that Africa has valuable contributions to offer to a mechanical civilization that totters on the brink of self-destruction. Africa, he believes, has vitality, rhythm, gaiety, and a wealth of spiritual insights which have escaped a speed-crazed, mechanized world. France and the West, in general, have much to offer Africa, he contends. A disciple of a cultural pluralism leading to human oneness, like his idol Teilhard de Chardin, Senghor envisages a world of brotherhood between whites and blacks as among men of all colors and cultures, combining widely diversified ethnic groups into one large human family.

Senghor's dream of this one human family combining the contributions of the many ethnic groups is a sort of Hegelian synthesis growing out of thesis and antithesis. The culture of the white world is interpreted as the thesis to which the culture of the African world becomes the antithesis. Out of the interaction, Senghor hopes that a new culture, a new world, may emerge.

The poem *"Prière aux masques"* is a melodious manifesto of his credo. It tells rhythmically of Africa's role in the brave new world of the poet's dream and summarizes his philosophy of a new Afro-French cultural exchange which can and should replace the exploitative relationships of the past to the mutual advantage of both peoples. Senghor sees beyond the death of the old order in Africa and in Europe to the rebirth of the new world. Africa and Europe, black and white, are joined together and share a mutual destiny for good or ill. The African brings his contribution which gives life to a dead world as yeast brings its vital contribution to the making of bread. The gift of the African will enrich the spirit — bringing rhythm, joy, memory, and the dance.

In *"A New York"* Senghor develops the same theme of the contribution of the black to the white culture, this time in the American setting. In the first section of the poem he describes the sterile, inhuman atmosphere of the great city. Then the poet sings of Harlem, which brings the beat of life into the city. Finally, he raises the note of celebration at the merging of black and white —*"laisse affleur sang noir dans ton sang . . ."* (let the black blood flow into your blood . . .).

Prière aux masques [6]

Masques! O Masques!
Masque noir, masque rouge, vous, masques blanc-et-noir,
Masques aux quatre points d'où souffle l'Esprit,
Je vous salue dans le silence!

Et pas toi le dernier, Ancêtre à tête de panthère.
Vous gardez ce lieu forclos à tout rire de femme, à tout
    sourire qui se fane;
Vous distillez cet air d'éternité où je respire l'air de mes
    Pères.
Masques aux visages sans masque, dépouillés de toute
    fossette comme de toute ride,
Qui avez composé ce portrait et ce visage mien penché
    sur l'autel de papier blanc
A votre image, écoutez-moi!
Voici que meurt l'Afrique des Empires — c'est l'agonie
    d'une princesse pitoyable —
Et aussi l'Europe à qui nous sommes liés par le nombril.
Fixez vos yeux immuables sur vos enfants que l'on
    commande,
Qui donnent, leur vie comme le pauvre son dernier
    vêtement.
Que nous répondions présents à la renaissance du
    Monde;
Ainsi le levain qui est nécessaire à la farine blanche.
Car qui apprendrait le rythme au monde défunt des
    machines et des canons?
Qui pousserait le cri de joie pour réveiller morts et
    orphelins à l'aurore?
Dites, qui rendrait la mémoire de vie à l'Homme aux
    espoirs éventrés.
Ils nous disent les hommes du coton, du café, de l'huile,
Ils nous disent les hommes de la Mort.
Nous sommes les hommes de la Danse, dont les pieds
    reprennent vigueur en frappant le sol dur.

[6] Senghor, "Prière aux masques," *Chants d'ombre*, p. 29.

Prayer to Masks [7]

MASKS! Masks!

Black mask, red mask, you white-and-black masks

Masks of the four points from which the Spirit blows

In silence I salute you!

Nor you the least, Lion-headed Ancestor

You guard this place forbidden to all laughter of women, to all smiles that fade

You distil this air of eternity in which I breathe the air of my Fathers.

Masks of unmasked faces, stripped of the marks of illness and the lines of age

You who have fashioned this portrait, this my face bent over the altar of white paper

In your own image, hear me!

The Africa of the empires is dying, see, the agony of a pitiful princess

And Europe too where we are joined by the navel.

Fix your unchanging eyes upon your children, who are given orders

Who give away their lives like the poor their last clothes.

Let us report present at the rebirth of the World

Like the yeast which white flour needs.

For who would teach rhythm to a dead world of machines and guns?

Who would give the cry of joy to wake the dead and the bereaved at dawn?

Say, who would give back the memory of life to the man whose hopes are smashed?

They call us men of coffee cotton oil

They call us men of death.

We are the men of the dance, whose feet draw new strength pounding the hardened earth.

[7] From *Selected Poems* by Léopold Sédar Senghor. Translated and Introduced by John Reed and Clive Wake, p. 9. Copyright © Oxford University Press 1964. Reprinted by permission of Atheneum Publishers, New York.

A New York [8]
(pour un orchestre de jazz: solo de trompette)

I

New York! D'abord j'ai été confondu par ta beauté, ces grandes filles d'or aux jambes longues.

Si timide d'abord devant tes yeux de métal bleu, ton sourire de givre

Si timide. Et l'angoisse au fond des rues à gratte-ciel

Levant des yeux de chouette parmi l'éclipse du soleil.

Sulfureuse ta lumière et les fûts livides, dont les têtes foudroient le ciel

Les gratte-ciel qui défient les cyclones sur leurs muscles d'acier et leur peau patinée de pierres.

Mais quinze jours sur les trottoirs chauves de Manhattan

— C'est au bout de la troisième semaine que vous saisit la fièvre en un bond de jaguar

Quinze jours sans un puits ni pâturage, tous les oiseaux de l'air

Tombant soudain et morts sous les hautes cendres des terrasses.

Pas un rire d'enfant en fleur, sa main dans ma main fraîche

Pas un sein maternel, des jambes de nylon. Des jambes et des seins sans sueur ni odeur.

Pas un mot tendre en l'absence de lèvres, rien que des coeurs artificiels payés en monnaie forte

Et pas un livre où lire la sagesse. La palette du peintre fleurit des cristaux de corail.

Nuits d'insomnie ô nuits de Manhattan! si agitées de feux follets, tandis que les klaxons hurlent des heures vides

Et que les eaux obscures charrient des amours hygiéniques, tels des fleuves en crue des cadavres d'enfants.

II

Voici le temps des signes et des comptes

New York! Or voici le temps de la manne et de l'hysope.

Il n'est que d'écouter les trombones de Dieu, ton coeur battre au rythme du sang ton sang.

J'ai vu dans Harlem bourdonnant de bruits de couleurs solennelles et d'odeurs flamboyantes

[8] Léopold Sédar Senghor, *Éthiopiques* (Paris: Editions du Seuil, 1956).

New York [9]
Jazz orchestra: solo trumpet

I

NEW YORK! At first your beauty confused me, and
your great long-legged golden girls.

I was so timid at first under your blue metallic eyes,
your frosty smile

So timid. And the disquiet in the depth of your sky-
scraper streets

Lifting up owl eyes in the sun's eclipse.

Your sulphurous light and the livid shafts (their heads
dumbfounding the sky)

Skyscrapers defying cyclones on their muscles of steel
and their weathered stone skins.

But a fortnight on the bald sidewalks of Manhattan

— At the end of the third week the fever takes you with
the pounce of a jaguar

A fortnight with no well or pasture, all the birds of
the air

Fall suddenly dead below the high ashes of the terraces.

No child's laughter blossoms, his hand in my fresh hand

No mother's breast. Legs in nylon. Legs and breasts with
no sweat and no smell.

No tender word for mouths are lipless. Hard cash buys
artificial hearts.

No book where wisdom is read. The painter's palette
flowers with crystals of coral.

Insomniac nights O nights of Manhattan, tormented by
fatuous fires, while the klaxons cry through the empty
hours

And dark waters bear away hygienic loves, like the
bodies of children on a river in flood.

II

It is the time of signs and reckonings

New York! It is the time of manna and hyssop.

Only listen to God's trombones, your heart beating to
the rhythm of blood your blood.

I have seen Harlem humming with sounds and solemn
colour and flamboyant smells

[9] From *Selected Poems* by Léopold Sédar Senghor. Trans-
lated and Introduced by John Reed and Clive Wake, pp. 78-79.
Copyright © Oxford University Press 1964. Reprinted by per-
mission of Atheneum Publishers, New York.

— C'est l'heure du thé chez le livreur-en-produits-phar-
maceutiques

J'ai vu se préparer la fête de la Nuit à la fuite de jour.
Je proclame la Nuit plus véridique que le jour.

C'est l'heure pure où dans les rues, Dieu fait germer la
vie d'avant mémoire

Tous les éléments amphibies rayonnants comme des
soleils.

Harlem Harlem! voici ce que j'ai vu Harlem Harlem!
Une brise verte de blés sourdre des pavés labourés
par les pieds nus de danseurs Dans

Croupes ondes de soie et seins de fers de lance, ballets
de nénuphars et de masques fabuleux

Aux pieds des chevaux de police, les mangues de l'amour
rouler des maisons basses.

Et j'ai vu le long des trottoirs, des ruisseaux de rhum
blanc des ruisseaux de lait noir dans le brouillard bleu
des cigares.

J'ai vu le ciel neiger au soir des fleurs de coton et des
ailes de séraphins et des panaches de sorciers.

Écoute New York! ô écoute ta voix mâle de cuivre ta voix
vibrante de hautbois, l'angoisse bouchée de tes larmes
tomber en gros caillots de sang

Écoute au loin battre ton coeur nocturne, rythme et sang
du tam-tam, tam-tam sang et tam-tam.

III

New York! je dis New York, laisse affluer le sang noir
dans ton sang

Qu'il dérouille tes articulations d'acier, comme une huile
de vie

Qu'il donne à tes ponts la courbes des croupes et la
souplesse des lianes.

Voici revenir les temps très anciens, l'unité retrouvée
la réconciliation du Lion du Taureau et de l'Arbre

L'idée liée à l'acte l'oreille au coeur le signe au sens.

Voilà tes fleuves bruissants de caïmans musqués et de
lamantins aux yeux de mirages. Et nul besoin d'inven-
ter les Sirènes.

Mais il suffit d'ouvrir les yeux à l'arc-en-ciel d'Avril

Et les oreilles, surtout les oreilles à Dieu qui d'un rire
de saxophone créa le ciel et la terre en six jours.

Et le septième jour, il dormit du grand sommeil négre.

— (It is tea-time for the man who delivers pharmaceutical products)

I have seen them preparing at flight of day, the festival of the Night. I proclaim there is more truth in the Night than in the day.

It is the pure hour when God sets the life before memory germinating in the streets

All the amphibious elements shining like suns.

Harlem Harlem! I have seen Harlem Harlem! A breeze green with corn springing from the pavements ploughed by the bare feet of dancers In

Crests and waves of silk and breasts of spearheads, ballets of lilies and fabulous masks

The mangoes of love roll from the low houses under the police horses' hooves.

I have seen down the sidewalks streams of white rum and streams of black milk in the blue haze of cigars.

I have seen the sky at evening snowing cotton flowers and wings of seraphim and wizard's plumes.

Listen, New York, listen to your brazen male voice your vibrant oboe voice, the muted anguish of your tears falling in great clots of blood

Listen to the far beating of your nocturnal heart, rhythm and blood of the drum, drum and blood and drum.

III

New York! I say to New York, let the black blood flow into your blood

Cleaning the rust from your steel articulations, like an oil of life

Giving your bridges the curve of the hills, the liana's suppleness.

See, the ancient times come again, unity is rediscovered the reconciliation of the Lion the Bull and the Tree

The idea is linked to the act the ear to the heart the sign to the sense.

See your rivers murmuring with musky caymans, manatees with eyes of mirage. There is no need to invent the Mermaids.

It is enough to open your eyes to the April rainbow

And the ears, above all the ears to God who with a burst of saxophone laughter created the heavens and the earth in six days.

And on the seventh day, he slept his great Negro sleep.

For all its social commentary, the poetry of Léopold Sédar Senghor attests to a high degree of craftsmanship. It is creative art at its best. First, M. Senghor brings to his art a great innate talent coupled with other artistic assets. Indeed, he captures the rhythms and music indigenous to his native Africa; and at times he combines several art forms: music, dance, and drama. Music is basic to his poetry. In his first collection *(recueil)*, *Chants d'ombre,* it is the drums *(les tamtams)* which provide the rhythm that is the key word *(mot-clé)* of his poetry. In *Éthiopiques,* African musical instruments are introduced, such as the *kôra* and the *balafong,* and later, as in *"A New York,"* the jazz orchestra with the trumpet and oboes predominating.

In *Nocturnes* the drum or *tamtam* loses its preponderant role in favor of flutes, the *khalam,* the *balafong,* and other orchestrated African instruments. These poems are generally read or recited to the accompaniment of the instruments named. Often in combining the several art forms, choir, dance, and painting, there is a dialogue between two or more of these forms, culminating in an orchestrated finale.

Though M. Senghor's poetic works are of the highest artistic merit, the poet, like most of his fellow Afro-French and Afro-American colleagues, sings in a minor key. The effective use of imagery and symbols is another tool in Senghor's artist's kit. Like other African poets, he makes frequent use of phallic symbols, as, for example, in his poem "Congo," dedicated to the great river, and in other poems in which he regards the earth as a woman, the farmer as the male mate, and farming as the act of sexual congress that leads to productivity. In "Congo," the river is a woman and the mountains symbolize the fertilizing male:

35

Congo [10]

Oho! Congo oho! Pour rythmer ton nom grand sur les
eaux sur les fleuves sur toute mémoire
Que j'émeuve la voix des koras, Koyaté! L'encre du
scribe est sans mémoire.

Oho! Congo couchée dans ton lit de forêts, reine sur
l'Afrique domptée
Que les phallus des monts portent haut ton pavillon
Car tu es femme par ma tête par ma langue, car tu es
femme par mon ventre
Mère de toute chose qui a nez, des crocodiles des hippo-
potames
Lamentins iguanes poissons oiseaux, mère des crues
nourrice des moissons.
Femme grande! eau tant ouverte à la rame et à l'étrave
des pirogues
Ma Saô ma femme aux cuisses furieuses aux longs bras
vêtus de nénuphars calmes
Femme précieuse d'ouzougou, corps d'huile imputrescible
à la peau de nuit diamantine.

Toi calme, déesse au sourire étale, sur l'élan vertigineux
de ton sang
O toi l'impaludée de ton lignage, délivre-moi de la
surrection de mon sang.
Tam-tam toi toi tam-tam des bonds de la panthère, de la
stratégie des fourmis
Des haines visqueuses au jour troisième surgies du poto-
poto des marais
Hâ! sur toute chose, du sol spongieux et des chants
savonneux de l'Homme-blanc
Mais délivre-moi de la nuit sans joie, et guette le silence
des forêts.
Donc que je sois le fût splendide et le bond de vingt-six
coudées
Dans l'alizé, sois la fuite de la pirogue sur le bouclier
lisse de ton ventre.

[10] Senghor, *Éthiopiques.*

Congo [11]

Lament for three koras and a balafong

Oho! Congo oho! I move the voices of the *koras* of
    Koyaté to make your great name their rhythm
Over the waters and rivers, over all I remember (the ink
    of the scribe remembers nothing).

Oho! Congo, asleep in your bed of forests, queen over
    Africa made subject
Phalli of mountains, hold high your pavilion
By my head by my tongue you are woman, you are
    woman by my belly
Mother of all things in whose nostrils is breath, mother
    of crocodiles and hippopotami
Manatees and iguanas, fishes and birds, mother of floods
    that suckle the harvests.
Great woman! Water wide open to the oar and the
    canoe's stem
My Sao my lover with maddened thighs, with long calm
    waterlily arms
Precious woman of *ouzougou,* body of imputrescible oil,
    skin of diamantine night.

Calm Goddess with your smile that rides the dizzy surges
    of your blood
Malarious by your descent, deliver me from the surrec-
    tion of my blood.
Drum drum you drum, from the panther's spring, the
    ant's strategy
From the viscous hates risen on the third day from the
    mud of the marshes
Ah! above all, from the spongy soil and the soapy songs
    of the Whiteman.
But deliver me from the night without joy and keep
    watch over the silence of the forests.
So I may become the splendid haft and the twenty-six
    cubit leap
In the wind, be the flight of the canoe on the supple
    surge of your belly.

[11] From *Selected Poems* by Léopold Sédar Senghor. Trans-
lated and Introduced by John Reed and Clive Wake, pp. 65-66.
Copyright © Oxford University Press 1964. Reprinted by per-
mission of Atheneum Publishers, New York.

Clairières de ton sein îles d'amour, collines d'ambre et de
gongo
Tanns d'enfance tanns de Joal, et ceux de Dyilôr en
Septembre
Et nuit d'Asnières en Septembre — il avait fait trop beau
trop doux.
Fleurs sereines de tes cheveux, pétales si blancs de ta
bouche
Surtout les doux propos à la néoménie, jusques à la
minuit du sang.
Délivre-moi de la nuit de mon sang, car guette le silence
des forêts.

Mon amante à mon flanc dont l'huile éburnéenne fait
docile mes mains mon âme.
Ma force s'érige dans l'abandon, mon honneur dans la
soumission
Et ma science dans l'instinct de ton rythme. Noue son
élan le coryphée
A la proue de son sexe à la vue du taureau, comme le
Tueur aux-yeux-de-torches.
Rythmez clochettes rythmez langues rythmez rames la
danse du Maître-des-rames.
Ah! elle est digne, sa pirogue, des choeurs triomphants
de Fadyoutt
Et je clame deux fois deux mains de tam-tams, quarante
vierges à chanter ses gestes.
Rythmez la flèche rutilante, la griffe à midi du Soleil
Rythmez, crécelles des cauris, les bruissements de la
Grande-Eau
Et la mort sur la crête de l'exultation, à l'appel irrécus-
able du gouffre.

Mais la pirogue renaîtra par les nymphéas de l'écume
Surnagera la douceur des bambous au matin transparent
du monde.

Clearings in your bosom islands of love, hills of amber and *gongo*

Seaflats of childhood of Joal, of Dyilor in September

Nights of Ermenonville in Autumn — the weather so fine and gentle.

Serene flowers of your hair, white petals of your mouth

And above all, gentle talk at the newmoon feast, drawn out till the midnight of the blood.

Deliver me from the night of my blood, for watch is kept by the silence of the forests.

My lover at my side, whose oil makes docile my hands my heart

My strength is set up in abandon, my honour in submission

And my wisdom in the instinct of your rhythm. The leader of the dance makes fast his vigour

To the prow of his sex, like the proud hunter of manatees.

Ring out bells, sing out tongues, beat out oars the dance of the Master of oars.

And his canoe is worthy of the triumphant choirs of Fadyoutt

And I call for twice two hands at the drums, for forty virgins to sing his deeds.

Beat the rhythm of the arrow glowing red, the Sun's claw at noon

Sound, cowrie-rattles, the rhythm of the rumble of Mighty Waters

Of death on the crest of exultation, the irrecusable call of the deep.

But the canoe is to be born again among the lilies of foam

To float above the sweetness of bamboos in the transparent morning of the world.

Two poems of Senghor are particularly significant and relevant today. They are the last two poems in the collection titled *Hosties Noires* [Black Hosts], i.e., Communion elements. The first is entitled *"Aux Soldats Négro Américains"* and is dedicated to Mercer Cook, former U.S. Ambassador to the West African republics of Niger and Senegal and an outstanding Africanist and professor of French as well as a longtime friend and translator of Senghor. The second, *"Prière de Paix"* [Prayer of Peace], is dedicated to Georges Pompidou, President of France and Senghor's schoolmate at the Lycée Louis-le-Grand in Paris, and his wife Claude. In *"Prière de Paix,"* the President of Senegal, speaking indirectly to the President of France, asks God's forgiveness for white Europe's wrongs to black Africa, and France is singled out for the Deity's special consideration.

The two poems follow.

Aux Soldats Négro-Américains [12]

A Mercer Cook

Je ne vous ai pas reconnus sous votre prison d'uniformes couleur de tristesse

Je ne vous ai pas reconnus sous la calebasse du casque sans panache

Je n'ai pas reconnu le hennissement chevrotant de vos chevaux de fer, qui boivent mais ne mangent pas.

Et ce n'est plus la noblesse des éléphants, c'est la lourdeur barbare des monstres des prétemps du monde.

Sous votre visage fermé, je ne vous ai pas reconnus.

J'ai touché seulement la chaleur de votre main brune, je me suis nommé: "Afrika!"

Et j'ai retrouvé le rire perdu, j'ai salué la voix ancienne et le grondement des cascades du Congo.

Frères, je ne sais si c'est vous qui avez bombardé les cathédrales, orgueil de l'Europe

Si vous êtes la foudre dont la main de Dieu a brûlé Sodome et Gomorrhe.

Non, vous êtes les messagers de sa merci, le souffle du Printemps après l'Hiver.

---

[12] Léopold Sédar Senghor, *Hosties Noires* (Paris: Editions du Seuil, 1945).

To the American Negro Soldiers [13]

To Mercer Cook

I did not recognize you in your prison of sad-coloured uniforms

I did not recognize you under that calabash helmet with no plume

I did not recognize the quavering whinny of your iron horses that drink but do not eat.

No longer the nobility of elephants but the barbaric clumsiness of monsters from the foretime of the world.

Under your closed faces I did not recognize you.

I only touched the warmth of your brown hand. I said my name, 'Afrika!'

And found again lost laughter, I greeted the ancient voice and the roar of the cascades of the Congo.

Brothers, I do not know if it was you who bombed the cathedrals, the pride of Europe

If you are the lightning that in God's hand burnt Sodom and Gomorrah.

No, you are the messengers of his mercy, breath of Spring after Winter.

[13] From *Selected Poems* by Léopold Sédar Senghor. Translated and Introduced by John Reed and Clive Wake, p. 47. Copyright © Oxford University Press 1964. Reprinted by permission of Atheneum Publishers, New York.

A ceux qui avaient oublié le rire — ils ne se servaient plus
que d'un sourire oblique

Qui ne connaissaient plus que la saveur salée des larmes
et l'irritante odeur du sang

Vous apportez le printemps de la Paix et l'espoir au
bout de l'attente.

Et leur nuit se remplit d'une douceur de lait, les champs
bleus du ciel se couvrent de fleurs, le silence chante
suavement.

Vous leur apportez le soleil. L'air palpite de murmures
liquides et de pépiements cristallins et de battement
soyeux d'ailes

Les cités aériennes sont tièdes de nids.

Par les rues de joie ruisselante, les garçons jouent avec
leurs rêves

Les hommes dansent devant leurs machines et se surpren-
nent à chanter.

Les paupières des écolières sont pétales de roses, les
fruits mûrissent à la poitrine des vierges

Et les hanches des femmes — oh! douceur — généreuse-
ment s'alourdissent.

Frères noirs, guerriers dont la bouche est fleur qui chante
—Oh! délice de vivre après l'Hiver — je vous salue
comme des messagers de paix.

For those who had forgotten laughter (using only an oblique smile)

Who had forgotten the salt taste of tears and the irritant smell of blood

You bring the springtime of Peace, hope at the end of waiting.

And their night fills with a sweetness of milk, the blue fields of the sky are covered with flowers, softly the silence sings.

You bring the sun. The air throbs with liquid murmurs and crystalline whistling and the silky beat of wings

Aerial cities are warm with nests.

Down streets running with joy, boys play with their dreams

Men dance before their machines, and catch themselves singing.

The eyelids of schoolgirls are rose petals, fruits ripen at the breasts of virgins

The hips of the women — O sweetness — grow full and heavy.

Black brothers, warriors whose mouths are singing flowers

— O delight to live after Winter — I greet you as the messengers of peace.

Prière de Paix [14]

(pour grandes orgues)

A Georges et Claude Pompidou

". . . Sicut et nos dimittimus debitoribus nostris."

I

Seigneur Jésus, à la fin de ce livre que je T'offre comme un ciboire de souffrances

Au commencement de la Grande Année, au soleil de Ta paix sur les toits neigeux de Paris

— Mais je sais bien que le sang de mes frères rougira de nouveau l'Orient jaune, sur les bords de l'Océan Pacifique que violent tempêtes et haines

Je sais bien que ce sang est la libation printanière dont les Grands-Publicains depuis septante années engraissent les terres d'Empire

Seigneur, au pied de cette croix — et ce n'est plus Toi l'arbre de douleur, mais au-dessus de l'Ancien et du Nouveau Monde l'Afrique crucifiée

Et son bras droit s'étend sur mon pays, et son côté gauche ombre l'Amérique

Et son coeur est Haïti cher, Haïti qui osa proclamer l'Homme en face du Tyran

Au pied de mon Afrique crucifiée depuis quatre cents ans et pourtant respirante

Laisse-moi Te dire, Seigneur, sa prière de paix et de pardon.

II

Seigneur Dieu, pardonne à l'Europe blanche!

Et il est vrai, Seigneur, que pendant quatre siècles de lumières, elle a jeté la bave et les abois de ses molosses sur mes terres

Et les chrétiens, abjurant Ta lumière et la mansuétude de Ton coeur

Ont éclairé leurs bivouacs avec mes parchemins, torturé mes talbés, déporté mes docteurs et mes maîtres-de-science.

---

[14] Senghor, *Hosties Noires*.

Prayer for Peace [15]

For grand organ

To Georges and Claude Pompidou

'. . . sicut et nos dimittimus debitoribus nostris.'

I

LORD JESUS, at the end of this book which I offer to Thee as a ciborium of sufferings

At the beginning of the Great Year, in the sun of Thy peace on the snow-covered roofs of Paris

— Though I know that the blood of my brothers will redden once more the yellow East, on the shores of the Pacific Ocean, desecrated by storms and hate

I know that this blood is the spring libation, for seventy years the Great Publicans have fattened with it the lands of Empire

Lord, at the foot of this cross — and it is no longer Thou who art the tree of suffering, but over the Old and New Worlds Africa crucified

And her right arm stretches over my country, and her left side shadows America

And her heart is beloved Haiti that dared proclaim Man to the Tyrant's face

At the foot of my Africa crucified for four hundred years yet breathing still

Let me say to Thee, Lord, her prayer of peace and pardon.

II

Lord God, forgive white Europe.

It is true Lord, that for four enlightened centuries, she has scattered the baying and slaver of her mastiffs over my lands

And the Christians, forsaking Thy light and the gentleness of Thy heart

Have lit their camp fires with my parchments, tortured my disciples, deported my doctors and masters of science.

[15] From *Selected Poems* by Léopold Sédar Senghor. Translated and Introduced by John Reed and Clive Wake, pp. 48-51. Copyright © Oxford University Press 1964. Reprinted by permission of Atheneum Publishers, New York.

Leur poudre a croulé dans l'éclair la fierté des tatas et des collines

Et leurs boulets ont traversé les reins d'empires vastes comme le jour clair, de la Corne de l'Occident jusqu'à l'Horizon oriental

Et comme des terrains de chasse, ils ont incendié les bois intangibles, tirant Ancêtres et génies par leur barbe paisible.

Et ils ont fait de leur mystère la distraction dominicale de bourgeois somnambules.

Seigneur, pardonne à ceux qui ont fait des Askia des maquisards, de mes princes des adjudants

De mes domestiques des boys et de mes paysans des salariés, de mon peuple, un peuple de prolétaires.

Car il faut bien que Tu pardonnes à ceux qui ont donné la chasse à mes enfants comme à des éléphants sauvages.

Et ils les ont dressés à coups de chicotte, et ils ont fait d'eux les mains noires de ceux dont les mains étaient blanches.

Car il faut bien que Tu oublies ceux qui ont exporté dix millions de mes fils dans les maladreries de leurs navires

Qui en ont supprimé deux cents millions.

Et ils m'ont fait une vieillesse solitaire parmi la forêt de mes nuits et la savane de mes jours.

Seigneur, la glace de mes yeux s'embue

Et voilà que le serpent de la haine lève la tête dans mon coeur, ce serpent que j'avais cru mort. . . .

III

Tue-le Seigneur, car il me faut poursuivre mon chemin, et je veux prier singulièrement pour la France.

Seigneur, parmi les nations blanches, place la France à la droite du Père.

Oh! je sais bien qu'elle aussi est l'Europe, qu'elle m'a ravi mes enfants comme un brigand du Nord des boeufs, pour engraisser ses terres à cannes et coton, car la sueur nègre est fumier.

Qu'elle aussi a porté la mort et le canon dans mes villages bleus, qu'elle a dressé les miens les uns contre les autres comme des chiens se disputant un os

Qu'elle a traité les résistants de bandits, et craché sur les têtes-aux-vastes-desseins.

Their powder has crumbled in a flash the pride of *tatas* and hills

And their bullets have gone through the bowels of vast empires like daylight, from the Horn of the West to the Eastern Horizon

They have fired the intangible woods like hunting grounds, dragged out Ancestors and spirits by their peaceable beards,

And turned their mystery into Sunday distraction for somnambulant bourgeois.

Lord, forgive them who turned the Askia into *maquisards,* my princes into sergeant-majors

My household servants into 'boys,' my peasants into wage-earners, my people into a working class.

For Thou must forgive those who have hunted my children like wild elephants,

And broken them in with whips, have made them the black hands of those whose hands were white.

For Thou must forget those who exported ten millions of my sons in the leperhouses of their ships

Who killed two hundred millions of them.

And have made for me a solitary old age in the forest of my nights and the savannah of my days.

Lord, the glasses of my eyes grow dim

And lo, the serpent of hatred raises its head in my heart, that serpent that I believed was dead.

III

Kill it Lord, for I must follow my way, and I would pray especially for France.

Lord, among the white nations, set France at the right hand of the Father.

O I know she too is Europe, that she has stolen my children like a brigand from the north to fatten her cornfields and cottonfields, for the sweat of the Negro is dung.

She too has brought death and guns into my blue villages, has set my people one against the other, like dogs fighting over a bone

Has treated those who resisted as bandits and spat upon the heads that held great schemes.

Oui, Seigneur, pardonne à la France qui dit bien la voie droite et chemine par les sentiers obliques

Qui m'invite à sa table et me dit d'apporter mon pain, qui me donne de la main droite et de la main gauche enlève la moitié.

Oui, Seigneur, pardonne à la France qui hait les occupants et m'impose l'occupation si gravement

Qui ouvre des voies triomphales aux héros et traite ses Sénégalais en mercenaires, faisant d'eux les dogues noirs de l'Empire

Qui est la République et livre les pays aux Grands-Concessionnaires

Et de ma Mésopotamie, de mon Congo, ils ont fait un grand cimetière sous le soleil blanc.

IV

Ah! Seigneur, éloigne de ma mémoire la France qui n'est pas la France, ce masque de petitesse et de haine sur le visage de la France

Ce masque de petitesse et de haine pour qui je n'ai que haine — mais je peux bien haïr le Mal

Car j'ai une grande faiblesse pour la France

Bénis ce peuple garrotté qui par deux fois sut libérer ses mains et osa proclamer l'avènement des pauvres à la royauté

Qui fit des esclaves du jour des hommes libres égaux fraternels

Bénis ce peuple qui m'a apporté Ta Bonne Nouvelle, Seigneur, et ouvert mes paupières lourdes à la lumière de la foi.

Il a ouvert mon coeur à la connaissance du monde, me montrant l'arc-en-ciel des visages neufs de mes frères.

Je vous salue mes frères: toi Mohamed Ben Abdallah, toi Razafymahatratra, et puis toi là-bas Pham-Manh-Tuong, vous des mers pacifiques et vous des forêts enchantées

Je vous salue tous d'un coeur catholique.

Ah! je sais bien que plus d'un de Tes messagers a traqué mes prêtres comme gibier et fait un grand carnage d'images pieuses.

Et pourtant on aurait pu s'arranger, car elles furent, ces images, de la terre à Ton ciel l'échelle de Jacob

Yes, Lord, forgive France that shows the right way, and goes by devious paths

Who invites me to her table and bids me bring my own bread, who gives with the right hand and takes away half with the left.

Yes Lord, forgive France who hates her occupiers and yet lays so heavy an occupation upon me

Who opens the triumphal way to heroes and treats the Senegalese as mercenaries, makes them the black watchdogs of Empire

Who is the Republic and grants whole countries to concessionary companies

And they, of my Riverland, of my Congo have made a great cemetery under the white sun.

IV

O Lord, take from my memory the France which is not France, mask of smallness and hatred upon the face of France

That mask of smallness and hatred for which I have hatred — yet I may well hate Evil

For I have a great weakness for France.

Bless this people who were tied and twice able to free their hands and proclaim the coming of the poor into the kingdom

Who turned the slaves of the day into men free equal fraternal

Bless this people who brought me Thy Good News, Lord, and opened my heavy eyelids to the light of faith.

Who opened my heart to the understanding of the world, showing me the rainbow of fresh faces that are my brothers.

I greet you my brothers: you Mohamed Ben Abdallah, you Razafymahatratra, and you Pham-Manh-Tuong, you from the pacific seas and you from the enchanted forests

I greet you all with a catholic heart.

Ah! I know that some of Thy messengers have tracked down my priests like game and made great destruction of holy images,

When we could have found an agreement for they were, those images, Jacob's ladder from the earth to Thy heaven

La lampe au beurre noir qui permet d'attendre l'aube, les étoiles qui préfigurent le soleil.
Je sais que nombre de Tes missionaires ont béni les armes de la violence et pactisé avec l'or des banquiers
Mais il faut qu'il y ait des traîtres et des imbéciles.

V

O bénis ce peuple, Seigneur, qui cherche son propre visage sous le masque et a peine à le reconnaître
Qui Te cherche parmi le froid, parmi la faim qui lui rongent os et entrailles
Et la fiancée pleure sa viduité, et le jeune homme voit sa jeunesse cambriolée
Et la femme lamente oh! l'oeil absent de son mari, et la mère cherche le rêve de son enfant dans les gravats.
O bénis ce peuple qui rompt ses liens, bénis ce peuple aux abois qui fait front à la meute boulimique des puissants et des tortionnaires.
Et avec lui tous les peuples d'Europe, tous les peuples d'Asie tous les peuples d'Afrique et tous les peuples d'Amérique
Qui suent sang et souffrances. Et au milieu de ces millions de vagues, vois les têtes houleuses de mon peuple.
Et donne à leur mains chaudes qu'elles enlacent la terre d'une ceinture de mains fraternelles.
DESSOUS L'ARC-EN-CIEL DE TA PAIX

Paris, janvier 1945.

The lamp fed with clear butter oil that let us await the dawn, the stars that prefigure the sun.

I know many of your missionaries have blessed the weapons of violence and come to terms with the gold of the bankers

But there will always be traitors and always fools.

V

O bless this people, Lord, who seek their own face under the mask and can hardly recognize it

Who seek Thee amidst cold and hunger that gnaw their bones and entrails

And the betrothed laments her widowhood and the young man sees his youth filched away

And the wife laments her husband's absent eye, and the mother picks over rubbish to find the dream of her child.

O bless this people that breaks its bonds, O bless this people at bay who face the bulimic pack of bullies and torturers.

And with them all the peoples of Europe, all the peoples of Asia, all the peoples of Africa, all the peoples of America

Who sweat blood and sufferings. And see, in the midst of these millions of waves, the sea-swell of the heads of my people.

And grant to their warm hands that they may clasp the earth in a girdle of brotherly hands

BENEATH THE RAINBOW OF THY PEACE.

3
Aimé Césaire

In her excellent book on Aimé Césaire and his works, in the *Poètes d'Aujourd'hui* series, Lilyan Kesteloot appraises the extraordinary talent of this Afro-French, West Indian poet as follows:

> Je ne vois pas dans l'histoire de la littérature française une personnalité qui ait à ce point intégré des éléments aussi divers que la conscience raciale, la création artistique et l'action politique. Je ne vois pas de personnalité aussi puissamment unifiée et à la fois aussi complexe que celle de Césaire. Et c'est là, sans doute, que réside le secret de l'exceptionnelle densité d'une poésie qui s'est, à un degré extrême, chargée de toute la cohérence d'une vie d'homme.[1]

> I do not see in the history of French literature a personality who has so highly integrated such diverse elements as racial consciousness, artistic creation, and political action. I do not see any personality so powerfully unified and at the same time so complex as that of Césaire. And, without doubt, therein resides the secret of the exceptional density of a poetry which has, to an extreme degree, taken on itself all the coherence of a man's life.

Paying eloquent tribute to Césaire's rare poetic gifts in his Préface to Césaire's first major collection, *Cahier d'un retour au pays natal,* the "high priest" of French surrealistic poetry, André Breton, who discovered Césaire during a visit to Martinique, has this to say in that Preface, titled *"Un grand poète noir"* [To a Great Black Poet]:

[1] Lilyan Kesteloot, *Aimé Césaire* (Paris: Editions Pierre Seghers, 1962), p. 9.

Et c'est un noir qui manie la langue française comme il n'est pas aujourd'hui un blanc pour la manier. Et c'est un noir celui qui nous guide aujourd'hui dans l'inexploré, établissant au fur et à mesure, comme en se jouant, les contacts qui nous font avancer sur des étincelles. Et c'est un noir qui est non seulement un noir mais *tout* l'homme, qui en exprime toutes les interrogations, toutes les angoisses, tous les espoirs et toutes les extases et qui s'imposera de plus en plus à moi comme le prototype de la dignité.

A black man it is who masters the French language as no white man can today. A black man it is who guides us today through unexplored lands building as he goes the contacts that will make us progress on sparks. A black man it is who embodies not simply the black race but *all* mankind, its queries and anxieties, its hopes and ecstasies and who will remain for me the symbol of dignity.[2]

Just who is this black poet who has elicited such flattering appraisals from persons best equipped to appreciate his genius? To understand Césaire's complexities and the magnitude of his anger, we are reminded by his biographer that one must understand the island which gave birth to him: Martinique, in the French West Indies, where dazzling luxury and wealth on the part of the few (whites) are in sharp contrast with the abject poverty of the masses (blacks) — where hunger, disease, and ignorance stalk the land — where former slavery and present-day exploitation have combined to crush the black masses of the population. This is especially true of Martinique, where Aimé Césaire was born in 1913, ". . . a miniature house which lodges in its guts of rotten wood dozens of rats, as well as the turbulence of my six brothers and sisters, a tiny cruel house whose intransigence infuriates the last days of the month . . ." (". . . *une maison minuscule qui abrite en ses entrailles de bois pourri des dizaines de rats et la turbulence de mes six frères et soeurs, une petite maison cruelle dont l'intransigeance affole nos fins de mois . . .").[3] His family was, however, in the "middle" *(moyen)* on the scale of local wretchedness, his father being, for a time at least, an "employee of the lower-echelon government" *(petit fonctionnaire)* in the town of Basse-Pointe.

[2] André Breton, "Preface: Un grand poète noir," in A. Césaire, *Cahier d'un retour au pays natal* [Return to my native land], tr. Emile Snyder (Paris: Présence Africaine, 1956), pp. 14-15.

[3] Aimé Césaire, *Cahier d'un retour au pays natal* [Return to my native land], tr. Emile Snyder (Paris: Présence Africaine, 1956), pp. 50-53.

Even worse than the material poverty afflicting the island was the spiritual and moral bankruptcy resulting from years of domination and exploitation: the complete resignation, loss of the will to resist, and the despair and constant fear of hunger, unemployment, and the like. Moreover, a color elite had developed among non-whites, which further aggravated the real blacks.

Thanks to native intelligence, industry, and promise, Césaire was to be sent to France to pursue his secondary and higher education. The former was acquired at the Lycée Louis-le-Grand, in Paris, where he met and began his lifelong friendship with Léopold Senghor. He then attended the Sorbonne and the École normale supérieure, the teacher-training school where to be admitted is an enviable distinction. Like Senghor, he graduated from both and was *agrégé* in literature. It was while Césaire was at the École normale supérieure, in 1935–1936, that this writer met him and introduced him to Sterling Brown via his poetic collection, *Southern Road*. Some years later, Césaire was to become mayor of Fort-de-France, capital of Martinique. After entering politics, he was elected delegate *(délégué)* to the Assemblée nationale in Paris; and in 1946, like Senghor, he was a member of the Assemblée constituante which framed the Constitution for the Fourth Republic in France (1946–1958).

Césaire's bitterness attracted him to the Communist party, a recognized political party in France's multiparty set-up, which he later abandoned. Ultimately, his ardent Communist activities made him somewhat unpopular among literary circles in France, where he still lives with his wife and daughter and continues to write.

A co-founder of *L'Étudiant Noir* in Paris, Césaire was also one of a group of Communist and surrealist West Indian students who founded in 1932 a magazine known as *Légitime Défense*.

Thus this black poet who, in the eyes of another great poet, possesses qualities of soul and genius which brought the two men together in a deep and abiding friendship also possesses a universality of interest and appeal which makes him the voice not only of his native Martinique but of all mankind. Indeed, Césaire's song is a social lament which elicits a ready response from all those who suffer from social, economic, and political injustices.

First of all, Césaire is a poet: he is essentially a singer of songs. His native sense of rhythm and his power to transform into poetry the commonest and even the ugliest aspects of life make of him a truly great poet. To quote André Breton again:

> . . . la poésie de Césaire, comme toute grande poésie et tout grand art, vaut au plus haut point par le pouvoir de transmutation, qu'elle met en oeuvre et qui consiste, à partir des matériaux les plus déconsidérés, parmi lesquels il faut compter les laideurs et les servitudes mêmes, à produire on sait assez que ce n'est plus l'or la pierre philosophale mais bien la liberte.

> Césaire's poetry, like any great poetry or art, draws its supreme value from its power of transmutation which consists in taking the most discredited materials, among which daily squalor and constraints, and ultimately producing neither gold nor the philosopher's stone any longer but freedom itself.[4]

Césaire's poetry, whose rhythm is suggestive of the weird and mysterious beat of the tom-tom, is replete with the exotic and luxuriant beauty inspired by the flora and fauna of the tropics. It excels in colorful and vivid imagery.

Behind the exquisite beauty of Césaire's verse there is a profound and prophetic meditation on the social injustices of which his people, especially in Martinique, are victims. The bard of Martinique sings of the wretchedness of colonial peoples and bemoans their exploitation by a handful of European parasites, who, frequently in defiance of the law, set themselves up as cruel, inhuman masters of an unhappy people forced to resign themselves to a status of virtual slavery. He sings of the evils of this system of colonization as they manifest themselves in the daily life and activities of his native island — in poverty, miserable housing, poor health, ignorance, superstition, and prejudice. He sings of ". . . the hungry West Indies, pitted with smallpox, dynamited with alcohol, stranded in the mud of this bay, in the dirt of this city sinisterly stranded" (". . . les Antilles qui ont faim, les Antilles grêlées de petite vérole, les Antilles dynamitées d'alcool, échoués dans la boue de cette baie, dans la poussière de cette ville sinistrement échouées").[5]

Césaire's major work, for our purposes, at least, is his *Cahier d'un retour au pays natal*, written in Paris in

[4] André Breton, *op. cit.*, pp. 18-19.
[5] Césaire, *Cahier d'un retour au pays natal*, pp. 30-31.

1939 on the eve of the poet's return to his native Martinique after completing his work at the École normale supérieure. This work was published in the review *Volonté* in 1939, but it did not attract attention until it was republished by Bordas in 1947. As the young poet makes ready to return to his native soil after a highly successful academic sojourn in Paris, he is haunted by the real and tragic vision of the West Indies inflicted with hunger, disease, alcoholism, and moral turpitude — fruits of a despicable, though doomed, system of economic exploitation and social abuse. He thinks particularly of his native city:

> Au bout du petit matin, cette ville inerte et ses au-delà de lèpres, de consomption, de famines, de peurs tapies dans les ravins, de peurs juchées dans les arbres, de peurs creusées dans le sol, de peurs en dérive dans le ciel, de peurs amoncelées et ses fumerolles d'angoisse.

> At the end of the dawn, this inert city, with its lepers, consumption, famines, fears hidden in ravines, fears perched in trees, fears sunk in the soil, fears drifting in the sky, accumulations of fears with their fumeroles of anguish.[6]

These conditions with which the poet's hometown is afflicted invariably breed social vices and warp human personality and destroy human souls. The poet reflects:

> Au bout du petit matin, l'échouage hétéroclite, les puanteurs exacerbées de la corruption, les sodomies monstrueuses de l'hostie et du victimaire, les coltis infranchissables du préjugé et de la sottise, les prostitutions, les hypocrisies, les lubricités, les trahisons, les mensonges, les faux, les concussions—l'essoufflement des lâchetés insuffisantes, l'enthousiasme sans ahan aux poussis surnuméraires, les avidités, les hystéries, les perversions, les arlequinades de la misère, les estropiements, les prurits, les urticaires, les hamacs tièdes de la dégénérescence. Ici la parade des risibles et scrofuleux bubons, les poutures de microbes très étranges, les poisons sans alexitère connu, les sanies de plaies bien antiques, les fermentations imprévisibles d'espèces putrescibles.[7]

> At the end of the dawn, the odd stranding, the exacerbated stench of corruption, the monstrous sodomies of the offering and the sacrificer, the dauntless prows of prejudice and stupidity, the prostitutions, the hypocrisies, the lubricities, the treasons, the lies, the frauds—the concussions, the breathlessness of half-hearted cowards, the smooth enthusiasms of budding bureaucrats, the avidities, hysterias, perversions, the harlequinades of misery, the injuries, itchings, urticarias, the dreary hammocks of degeneracy. Here the parade of contemptible and scrofulous bubos, the gluttony of very strange microbes, the poisons for which there are no known alexins, the pus of very ancient wounds, the unforeseeable fermentations of species destined to decay.[8]

[6] *Ibid., pp.* 34-35.   [7] *Ibid.*, pp. 39, 41.   [8] *Ibid.*, pp. 38, 40.

Further in his dream of his return home, M. Césaire depicts the advent of Christmas in his native city. His reminiscences on this most beautiful of all Christian celebrations are all the more vivid because of the contrasts which they evoke between the economic extremes of the city. He announces the approach of Christmas in high poetic images:

> Et le temps passait vite, très vite.
> Passés août où les manguiers pavoisent de toutes leurs lunules, septembre l'accoucheur de cyclones, octobre le flambeur de cannes, novembre qui ronronne aux distilleries, c'était Noël qui commençait.

> And quickly, time went by.
> From August, when the mango-trees were decked with lunulas, to September, midwife of hurricanes, to October, incendiary of sugar canes, then November, purring in the distilleries, and suddenly Christmas was there.[9]

Then he depicts the joy that reigns habitually in the city at Christmas time:

> . . . et le bourg n'est plus qu'un bouquet de chants, et l'on est bien à l'intérieur, et l'on en mange du bon, et l'on en boit du réjouissant et il y a du boudin, celui étroit de deux doigts qui s'enroule en volubile, celui large et trapu, le bénin à goût de serpolet, le violent à incandescence pimenteé, et du café brûlant et de l'anis sucré et du punch au lait, et le soleil liquide des rhums, et toutes sortes de bonnes choses qui vous imposent autoritairement les muqueuses ou vous les distillent en ravissements, ou vous les tissent de fragrances, et l'on rit, et l'on chante. . . .

> . . . the little town is now only a bouquet of songs: you are well inside, you have good things to eat, wine to drink, and there are sausages, one kind is thin as two fingers tightly wound, the other big and dumpy, the soft kind tastes of thyme, the strong of red-hot spice, there is burning coffee and sugary anise, punch with milk, and the liquid sun of rum, and all sorts of good things which despotically work on your mucous membrane, distilling delights or weaving fragrances, and you laugh and sing. . . .[10]

But all these good things associated with the celebration of Christmas were reserved for the fortunate few in Basse-Pointe, the poet's native city. The observance of Christmas in the poet's own family contrasted sharply with the affluence and abundance of good things *(bonnes choses)* described above. He remembers his family abode, rat-infested and dilapidated in an ill-smelling, unsanitary street, as the scene of a

[9] *Ibid.*, pp. 44-45.
[10] *Ibid.*, pp. 46-47.

laborious mother tirelessly pedaling a Singer sewing machine in order to feed her numerous brood, while his indolent, irascible, and sickly father sat idly by. To such people, Christmas was hardly any different from any other day. The poet remembers this scene in these words:

> Au bout du petit matin, une autre petite maison qui sent très mauvais dans une rue très étroite, une maison minuscule qui abrite en ses entrailles de bois pourri des dizaines de rats et la turbulence de mes six frères et soeurs, une petite maison cruelle dont l'intransigeance affole nos fins de mois et mon père fantasque grignoté d'une seule misère, je n'ai jamais su laquelle, qu'une imprévisible sorcellerie assoupit en mélancolique tendresse ou exalte en hautes flammes de colère; et ma mère dont les jambes pour notre faim inlassable pédalent, pédalent de jour, de nuit, je suis même réveillé la nuit par ces jambes inlassables qui pédalent la nuit et la morsure âpre dans la chair molle de la nuit d'une Singer que ma mère pédale, pédale pour notre faim et de jour et de nuit.[11]

> At the end of the dawn, there is another tiny house stinking in the narrow street, a miniature house which lodges in its guts of rotten wood dozens of rats, as well as the turbulence of my six brothers and sisters, a tiny cruel house whose intransigence infuriates the last days of the month and my fantastic father chewed by a certain ailment, I never discovered what, my father whom an unanticipated sorcery makes drowsy with melancholy sweetness or exalts to the high flames of anger; and my mother, whose limbs, in the service of our tireless hunger, pedal, pedal, day and night, I am even awakened at night by those tireless limbs which pedal the night, by the bitter punctures in the soft flesh of the night made by the Singer machine my mother pedals, pedals for our hunger day and night.[12]

As the time for the poet's return approaches, he takes inventory of the rupture, which has developed during his stay in France, between him and his people, not only the relatives in the smelly little house but also all men of color similarly situated, and he seeks to repair that rupture. The first step in the process of repair is to destroy his refound cowardice *(lâcheté retrouvée)* which revealed itself to the poet one day when, on a Paris tramway, he had renounced his racial allegiance and solidarity with "a comical and ugly Negro" *(un nègre comique et laid)* whose presence was a source of embarrassment to the poet in the occidental setting so unsympathetic with this comical Negro (an incident described earlier). This impetuous and thoughtless decision was foolish, the poet concludes, and he must ac-

[11] *Ibid.*, pp. 51, 53.
[12] *Ibid.*, pp. 50, 52.

cept all that is characteristic of even the most backward of his people, all that has been imposed upon them by years of disease, poverty, and ignorance. All this he must accept as his heritage, and he must identify himself fervently with the cause and fate of Negroes. This he does: "*J'accepte, j'accepte tout cela . . . [toute cette Négritude]. . . .*" [13] He accepts the bad along with the good, but he does it in the conviction that the future holds a promise of liberation, of complete and real freedom for his people and for all peoples. He believes that the conquest of liberty has only begun: ". . . but the work of man has only begun . . . and there is room for all at the rendez-vous of conquest" ("*. . . l'oeuvre de l'homme vient seulement de commencer . . . et il est place pour tous au rendez-vous de la conquête*").[14]

The Negro, Césaire believes, is destined to have a part in mankind's liberation from "this serfdom of our time," a liberation of mind and body. As a poet, M. Césaire is resolved to fight for the former, and as a politician he is in the thick of the struggle for social and economic liberation. In his poem "*A l'Afrique*" he looks into his poetic crystal ball and foresees a pestilence that will depopulate the West, and he exhorts the peasants, with a philosophy suggestive of Voltaire's "cultivate your garden" (*cultivez votre jardin*), to continue to strike the earth, identifying himself with the toilers of the land, the tillers of the soil.

The caustic candor and cutting irony of the selection that follows point up the characteristic rage of Césaire when he is forced to defend blacks against the whites who have victimized them, reduced them to a status of social and economic inferiority, and then castigated them for being "inferior," for not having excelled as inventors, discoverers, explorers, philosophers, scholars, and so forth.

> Ceux qui n'ont inventé ni la poudre ni la boussole
> ceux qui n'ont jamais su dompter la vapeur ni l'électricité
> ceux qui n'ont exploré ni les mers ni le ciel
> mais ils savent en ses moindres recoins le pays de souffrance
> ceux qui n'ont connu de voyages que de déracinements
> ceux qui se sont assoupis aux agenouillements

[13] *Ibid.*, p. 137.
[14] *Ibid.*, pp. 138-141.

ceux qu'on domestiqua et christianisa
ceux qu'on inocula d'abâtardissement
tam-tams de mains vides
tam-tams inanes de plaies sonores
tam-tams burlesques de trahison tabide [15]

Those who invented neither powder nor compass
those who never tamed steam or electricity
those who did not explore sea or sky
  but they know in their innermost depths
  the country of suffering
those who knew of voyages only when uprooted
those who are made supple by kneelings
those domesticated and Christianized
those inoculated with degeneracy
tom-toms of empty hands
tom-toms of sounding wounds
burlesque tom-toms of treason.[16]

The *Cahier d'un retour* is above all a song, a lament, perhaps the greatest lyrical creation of our time. No lesser than M. André Breton has characterized it as "the greatest lyrical monument of our times" *("le plus grand monument lyrique de ce temps")*.[17]

Truly, M. Césaire, equipped with all that he could learn from the white man and his civilization, belongs, at least as far as his literary genius is concerned, body and soul to the vast collectivity of the proletariat, to the millions of laborers whose voice he becomes as he sings their joys and sorrows, their tribulations and aspirations. And Césaire's voice is in truth, as M. Breton has described it, "beautiful as nascent oxygen" *("belle comme l'oxygène naissant")*.[18]

As Lilyan Kesteloot puts it, *"Le Cahier* is a decisive date in the birth of black consciousness, and it has for twenty years served as a standard for the revolutionary youth of colonized countries," [19] whether in Africa or the West Indies or elsewhere. It may well be studied by black youth today in their efforts to set the current struggle in historical perspective. Alioune Diop characterizes this work as "the sum-total of Negro revolt against European history" *("la somme de la révolte nègre contre l'histoire européenne")*.[20]

[15] Césaire, *Cahier d'un retour au pays natal*, p. 111.
[16] *Ibid.*, p. 110.
[17] André Breton, *op. cit.*, pp. 16-17.
[18] *Ibid.*, pp. 26-27.
[19] Translated from Kesteloot, *Aimé Césaire*, p. 25.
[20] *Ibid.*

At once an epic and a lyrical poem, it defies classification as a poetic creation. Like the medieval literary form *(chante-fable)*, there is an alternation of verse with prose passages. It is unique, resembling only itself. Its surrealism is often hard to penetrate and to interpret. But where its social commentary is clear — which often it is not, thanks to surrealistic verbiage — it is a scathing denunciation of European colonialism and an eloquent apology for the dignity of man and his equality with all his fellowmen.

4
Léon-G. Damas

Co-founder with Senghor and Césaire of the *Négritude* school, Léon-G. Damas was born in Cayenne, Guyane (French Guiana), South America. After completing his secondary studies at the Lycée Schoelcher in Fort-de-France, Martinique, he went on to Paris, where he studied law and met Césaire and Senghor. In Paris, Damas was an habitué of all the places frequented by blacks from many countries of the world who had been attracted to this intellectual "Mecca" and bastion of individual freedom: Negro Americans, Senegalese, Congolese, Madagascans, Papous, West Indians, and others — students, writers, entertainers, workers, and so forth. Being a poor student, M. Damas lived intensely the intellectual and moral tragedy of his race, undergoing the identity crisis common to all his fellow blacks. His poetic sensitivity made him all the more vulnerable to that tragedy.

Damas's poetic works include *Pigments* (1937), *Graffiti,* and *Black Label.* His poetry, in contrast to that of Césaire and Senghor, is unsophisticated. It finds expression through everyday words, common or noble, most often those words and expressions of the common people, colored at times by an outmoded gracefulness and the use of certain Creole terms, and all of it subjected to the rhythm of the *tam tam,* for with Damas, rhythm takes precedence over melody. Being unsophisticated,

Damas's poetry is direct, brutish, and at times brutal; and not infrequently it is charged with an emotion disguised as humor, a characteristically Negro humor that has been the black man's saving grace in a harsh and cruel world in which he has had, for years, no other defense or technique of survival. That cruel, white-dominated world and the Negro's helplessness in it are dramatically depicted in the following poem taken from the collection entitled *Pigments:*

Ils sont venus ce soir [1]

Ils sont venus ce soir où le
tam
   tam
      roulait de
         rythme en
            rythme
               la frénésie
des yeux
la frénésie des mains la frénésie
des pieds de statues
DEPUIS
combien de MOI
sont morts
depuis qu'ils sont venus ce soir où le
tam
   tam
      roulait de
         rythme en
            rythme
               la frénésie
des yeux
la frénésie des mains la frénésie
des pieds de statues.

[1] Léon-G. Damas, *Pigments* (Paris: Présence Africaine, 1962).

They Came This Evening

They came this evening when the
tom-
   tom
      was rolling from
         rhythm to rhythm
            the frenzy
of the eyes
the frenzy of the hands, the frenzy
of the feet of statues.
SINCE
how many of ME
have died
since they came this evening when the
tom-
   tom
      was rolling from
         rhythm to rhythm
            the frenzy
of the eyes
the frenzy of the hands, the frenzy
of the feet of statues?

As for *Négritude* in Damas, the following poems are characteristic:

Limbé [2]

Rendez-les-moi mes poupées noires
qu'elles dissipent
l'image des catins blêmes marchands d'amour
qui s'en vont viennent
sur le boulevard de mon ennui

Rendez-les-moi mes poupées noires
qu'elles dissipent
l'image sempiternelle
l'image hallucinante
des fantoches empilés fessus
dont le vent porte au nez la misère
misèricorde

Donnez-moi l'illusion que je n'aurai plus à contenter
le besoin étale
des miséricordes ronflant
sous l'inconscient dédain
du monde

Rendez-les-moi mes poupées noires que je joue avec elles
les jeux naïfs de mon instinct
rester à l'ombre de ses lois
recouvrer mon courage
mon audace
me sentir moi-même
nouveau moi-même de ce que hier j'étais
hier
   sans complexité
     hier
quand est venue l'heure du déracinement

Le sauront-ils jamais cette rancune de mon coeur
à l'oeil de ma méfiance ouvert trop tard
ils ont cambriolé l'espace qui était mien
la coutume les jours la vie
la chanson le rythme l'effort
le sentier l'eau la case
la terre enfumée grise
la sagesse les mots les palabres

[2] *Ibid.*

Spleen

Give me back my black dolls.
Let them dispel the image of the livid tarts of the
    merchants of love
who come and go on the boulevard of my boredom.

Give me back my black dolls.
Let them dispel
the never-ceasing image,
the hallucinating image,
of the heaped puppets
whose pitiable wretchedness the wind brings to the
    nostrils.

Give me back the illusion that I shall no longer have
    to satisfy
the meat-stall need
of the mercies roaring
under the unconscious disdain
of the world.

Give me back my black dolls that I may play with them
the naive games of my instinct,
to remain in the shadow of its laws,
to recover my courage,
my audacity,
to feel myself
[a] new myself of what yesterday I was
yesterday
   without complexity;
     yesterday,
when came the hour of the uprooting.

Will they ever know this rancor of my heart
to the eye of my mistrust too late opened?
they have [burgled] ransacked the space that was mine,
the custom, the days, the life
the song, the rhythm, the effort,
the path, the water, the cabin
the gray, fertilized earth;
the wisdom, the words, the palaver,

les vieux
la cadence les mains la mesure les mains
les piétinements le sol

Rendez-les-moi mes poupées noires
mes poupées noires
poupées noires
noires.

the old
the cadence, the hands, the measure, the hands,
the trampling the soil.

Give me back my black dolls —
my black dolls,
black dolls,
dolls.

La Complainte du Nègre [3]

Ils me l'ont rendue la vie plus lourde et lasse
la liberté m'est une douleur affreuse
mes aujourd'hui ont chacun sur mon jadis
de gros yeux qui roulent de rancoeur de
honte

Les jours inexorablement tristes jamais n'ont
cessé d'être à la mémoire de ce que fut
ma vie tronquée
Va encore mon hébétude du temps jadis
de
coups de corde noueux de corps calcinés
de l'orteil au dos calcinés
de chair morte de tisons de fer rouge de bras
brisés sous le fouet qui se déchaîne sous le fouet qui
fait
marcher la plantation s'abreuver de sang
de mon sang de sang la sucrerie
et la bouffarde du commandeur craner au ciel.

[3] *Ibid.*

The Negro's Lament

They made my life more heavy and tired.
Freedom is for me a frightful suffering;
My todays have on each of my yesterdays
big eyes that roll with rancor, with shame.

The inexorably sad days have never
ceased to be at the remembrance of what was
my truncated life.
Go still my hebetude [dazed, stunned condition]
   of yesteryear,
of
whipping with a knotted rope, of charred bodies
from the big toe to the burned back
of dead flesh, of brands of red-hot fire, of arms
broken under the whip which is unleashed, under the
   whip
which makes one walk the plantation to drench itself
   with blood
of my blood, of blood, the sugar refinery
and the tobacco-pipe of the commander to swagger
   in heaven.

The following poem reveals particularly the identity crisis of the African or other black transplanted to a European milieu, where he is forced to renounce, for a time, at least, his ancestral culture and native dress and to live the life of "an uprooted misfit" *(déraciné)*.

Solde [4]

J'ai l'impression d'être ridicule
dans leurs souliers dans leur smoking
dans leur plastron dans leur faux col
dans leur monocle dans leur melon

J'ai l'impression d'être ridicule
avec mes orteils qui ne sont pas faits pour
transpirer du matin jusqu'au soir qui déshabille
avec l'emmaillotage qui m'affaiblit les membres
et enlève à mon corps sa beauté de cache-sexe

J'ai l'impression d'être ridicule
avec mon cou en cheminée d'usine
avec ces maux de tête qui cessent
chaque fois que je salue quelqu'un

J'ai l'impression d'être ridicule
dans leurs salons dans leurs manières
dans leurs courbettes dans leurs formules
dans leur multiple besoin de singeries

J'ai l'impression d'être ridicule
avec tout ce qu'ils racontent
jusqu'à ce qu'ils vous servent l'après-midi un peu d'eau
    chaude
et des gâteaux enrhumés

J'ai l'impression d'être ridicule
avec les théories qu'ils assaisonnent
au goût de leurs besoins de leurs passions
de leurs instincts ouverts la nuit en forme de paillasson.

J'ai l'impression d'être ridicule
parmi eux complice parmi eux souteneur
parmi eux égorgeur les mains effroyablement rouges
du sang de leur civilisation.

[4] *Ibid.*

Clearance

I have the impression of being ridiculous
in their shoes, in their tuxedos;
in their stiff shirt-front, in their collar,
in their monocle, in their derby hat.

I have the impression of being ridiculous
with my toes which are not made for
perspiring from morning to night, which undresses
with the swaddling which weakens my limbs
and takes away from my body its fig-leaf beauty.

I have the impression of being ridiculous
with my neck like a factory smokestack
with my headaches which stop
each time I greet someone.

I have the impression of being ridiculous
in their drawing rooms, in their manners,
in their bowing, in their formalities,
in their multiple need of imitations.

I have the impression of being ridiculous
with all that they recount
until they serve you in the afternoon a little hot water
and some cold cakes.

I have the impression of being ridiculous
with the theories that they season
to the taste of their needs, of their passions,
of their instincts opened at night in the form of a
   doormat.

I have the impression of being ridiculous
among them, accessory among them, pimp
among them, a cutthroat with frightfully bloody hands,
with the blood of their civilization.

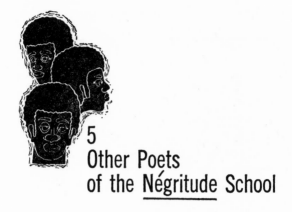

5
Other Poets
of the Négritude School

Guy Tirolien

Guy Tirolien was born in 1917 at Pointe-à-Pitre, Guadeloupe, (French West Indies), where he graduated from the Lycée of Pointe-à-Pitre. Afterward he served in Black Africa as Administrator of Colonies, under French rule. It was, however, before he set foot on African soil that he threw himself into the cultural struggle of the new Negro.

Tirolien's *"Prière d'un petit enfant nègre"* and *"L'âme du noir pays"* were published in 1943. These poems are carried on the following pages.

Prière d'un petit enfant nègre [1]

Seigneur je suis très fatigué.

Je suis né fatigué.

Et j'ai beaucoup marché depuis le chant du coq

Et le morne est bien haut qui mène à leur école.

Seigneur, je ne veux plus aller à leur école,

Faites, je vous en prie, que je n'y aille plus.

Je veux suivre mon père dans les ravines fraîches

Quand la nuit flotte encore dans le mystère des bois

Où glissent les esprits que l'aube vient chasser.

Je veux aller pieds nus par les rouges sentiers

Que cuisent les flammes de midi,

Je veux dormir ma sieste au pied des lourds manguiers,

Je veux me réveiller

Lorsque là-bas mugit la sirène des blancs

Et que l'Usine

Sur l'océan des cannes

Comme un bateau ancrée

Vomit dans la campagne son équipage nègre . . .

Seigneur, je ne veux plus aller à leur école,

Faites, je vous en prie, que je n'y aille plus.

Ils racontent qu'il faut qu'un petit nègre y aille

Pour qu'il devienne pareil

Aux messieurs de la ville

Aux messieurs comme il faut.

Mais moi je ne veux pas

Devenir, comme ils disent,

Un monsieur de la ville,

Un monsieur comme il faut.

Je préfère flâner le long des sucreries

Où sont les sacs repus

Que gonfle un sucre brun autant que ma peau brune.

Je préfère vers l'heure où la lune amoureuse

Parle bas à l'oreille des cocotiers penchés

Écouter ce que dit dans la nuit

La voix cassée d'un vieux qui raconte en fumant

Les histoires de Zamba et de compère Lapin

Et bien d'autres choses encore

Qui ne sont pas dans les livres.

Les nègres, vous le savez, n'ont que trop travaillé.

Pourquoi faut-il de plus apprendre dans des livres

[1] Guy Tirolien, "Prière d'un petit enfant nègre," as quoted in Léopold S. Senghor, *Anthologie de la nouvelle poèsie nègre et Malgache* (Paris: Presses Universitaires de France, 1948), pp. 86-87.

Prayer of a Little Negro Child

Lord, I am very tired.
I was born tired.
And I have walked since the cock crew.
And high is the bluff that leads to their school.
Lord, I don't want to go to their school any more,
Help me to go there no more.
I want to follow my father into the cool ravines
When night still floats in the mystery of the woods,
Where slip the spirits which the dawn comes and chases.
I want to go barefoot through the red paths
That are cooked by the noonday sun.
I want to sleep my siesta at the foot of heavy mango trees.
I want to awaken
When the white man's siren sounds over there
And when the Factory
Over the ocean of cane fields,
Like an anchored boat,
Vomits its Negro crew into the countryside . . .
Lord, I do not want to go to their school any more.
Fix it so I don't have to go there any more.
They say that a little Negro must go there
In order to become like
The gentlemen of the city.
Like true gentlemen.
But I do not want
to become, as they say,
A gentleman.
I prefer to stroll along the sugar refineries
Where the full sacks are
That bulge with a sugar brown like my skin.
I prefer, around the time when the lovers' moon
Whispers in the ear of bent-over coconut workers,
To listen to what the broken voice of an old man,
Who tells, as he smokes, the stories of Sambo and
Brother Rabbit, says in the night.
And many other things that are not in books.
Negroes, you know, have worked but too much.
Why must one, in addition, learn from books,

Qui nous parlent de choses qui ne sont point d'ici?
Et puis elle est vraiment trop triste leur école,
Triste comme
Ces messieurs de la ville,
Ces messieurs comme il faut
Qui ne savent plus danser le soir au clair de lune
Qui ne savent plus marcher sur la chair de leurs pieds
Qui ne savent plus conter les contes aux veillées.
Seigneur, je ne veux plus aller à leur ecole.

Which speak of things that are not of here?
And then their school is really too sad,
Sad like those gentlemen of the city
Those "gentlemen"
Who can no longer dance in the moonlight,
Who can no longer walk on the flesh of their feet,
Who can no longer tell tales at wakes.
Lord, I no longer want to go to their school.

L'âme du noir pays [2]

Tes seins de satin noir rebondis et luisants
tes bras souples et longs dont le lissé ondule
ce blanc sourire
des yeux
dans l'ombre du visage
éveillent en moi ce soir
les rythmes sourds
les mains frappées
les lentes mélopées
dont s'enivrent là-bas au pays de Guinée
nos soeurs
noires et nues
et font lever en moi
ce soir
des crépuscules nègres lourds d'un sensuel émoi
car
l'âme du noir pays où dorment les anciens
vit et parle
ce soir
en la force inquiète le long de tes reins creux
en l'indolente allure d'une démarche fière
qui laisse quand tu vas
traîner après tes pas
le fauve appel des nuits
que dilate et qu'emplit
l'immense pulsation des tam-tams en fièvre
car
en ta voix surtout
ta voix au timbre nostalgique
ta voix qui se souvient
vibre et pleure
ce soir
l'âme du noir pays où dorment les anciens.

[2] Guy Tirolien, "L'âme du noir pays," as quoted in Senghor, *op. cit.*, pp. 87-88.

The Soul of the Black Country

Your breasts of black satin, firm and shiny,
Your long and supple arms whose smoothness undulates;
That white smile,
Eyes,
In the shadow of your face
Awaken in me tonight
The heavy rhythms.
Hands clapped,
The slow chant,
which intoxicates over there in the country of Guinea
Our sisters
Black and nude
And cause to rise in me
Tonight
Negro dusks heavy with a sensual emotion
for
the soul of the black country where sleep the ancients,
lives and speaks
Tonight
In the restless strength along your hollow back
In the lazy stride of a proud step
which leaves when you go
to drag after your steps
the wild call of the nights
which the immense pulsation of the feverish drums
dilates and fills
In your voice especially
your voice with the nostalgic timbre,
your voice which remembers,
vibrates and weeps
Tonight
The soul of the black country where sleep the ancients.

Paul Niger

Paul Niger was born in 1917 in Basse-Terre, Guade-loupe, where he received his secondary education. Like his fellow West Indians *(antillais)*, Césaire, Damas, and Guy Tirolien, he went to Paris for his higher education. It was his contact with Mother Africa which brought forth his poetic talent, which revealed itself in poems at once violent and tender, like the land of his ancestors. The following poem is an example:

Je n'aime pas l'Afrique [3]

"J'aime ce pays, disait-il, on y trouve nourriture, obéis-sance, poulets à quatre sous, femmes à cent, et 'bien Missié' pour pas plus cher.

Le seul problème, ajoutait-il, ce sont les anciens tirail-leurs et les métis et les lettrés qui discutent les ordres et veulent se faire élire chefs de village."

Moi, je n'aime pas cette Afrique-là.

L'Afrique des "naya"
L'Afrique des "makou"
L'Afrique des "a bana"
L'Afrique des yesmen et des beni — oui — oui.
L'Afrique des hommes couchés attendant comme une grâce le réveil de la botte.

L'Afrique des boubous flottant comme des drapeaux de capitulation de la dysenterie, de la peste, de la fièvre jaune et des chiques (pour ne pas dire de la chicotte).

L'Afrique de "l'homme du Niger," l'Afrique des plaines désolées.

Labourées d'un soleil homicide, l'Afrique des pagnes obscènes et des muscles noués par l'effort du travail forcé.

L'Afrique des négresses servant l'alcool d'oubli sur le plateau de leurs lèvres.

L'Afrique des boys suceurs, des maîtresses de douze ans, des seins au balancement rythmé de papayes trop mûres et des ventres ronds comme une calebasse en saison sèche.

L'Afrique des Paul MORAND et des André DEMAISON.

Je n'aime pas cette Afrique-là.

---

[3] Paul Niger, "Je n'aime pas l'Afrique," as quoted in Senghor, *op. cit.*, pp. 93-100.

I Do Not Like Africa

"I like that country," he was saying, "one finds there food, obedience, chickens at four pennies, women at one hundred, and 'bien Missié' very cheap.

"The only problem," he added, "is the former sharp-shooters and the half-breeds and the lettered people who discuss the orders and want to get elected village chiefs."

Me, I do not like *that* Africa!

The Africa of the *"nayas"* (here)

The Africa of the *"makou"* (silence)

The Africa of the *"a bana"* (ended)

The Africa of the yesmen and the blessed yes-yes.

The Africa of men lying down awaiting like a grace to be awakened by a kick.

The Africa of *boubous* [loose, toga-like garments] floating like flags of surrender, of dysentery, of the plague, of yellow fever, and of chiggers. . . .

The Africa of "the man from Niger," the Africa of desolate plains.

Farmed by [a] murderous sun, the Africa of obscene loincloths, of muscles knotted by the effort of forced labor.

The Africa of Negro women serving the alcohol of forgetfulness on their plateau lips.

The Africa of sucking boys, of twelve-year-old mistresses, of breasts swaying rhythmically like overripe papayas, and of bellies rounded like gourds in the dry season.

The Africa of the Paul Morands and the André Demaisons.

I do not like that Africa.

[Here begins a biblical parable that reaches peaks of sacrilege.]

Dieu, un jour descendu sur la terre, fut désolé de l'attitude des créatures envers la création. Il ordonna le déluge, et germa, de la terre ressurgie, une semence nouvelle.

L'arche peupla le monde et lentement

Lentement

L'humanité monta des âges sans lumière aux âges sans repos.

Il avait oublié l'Afrique.

Christ racheta l'homme mauvais et bâtit son Église à Rome.

Sa voix fut entendue dans le désert. L'Église sur la Société, la Société sur l'Église, l'une portant l'autre.

Fondèrent la civilisation où les hommes, dociles à l'antique sagesse, pour apaiser les anciens dieux, pas morts.

Immolèrent tous les dix ans quelques millions de victimes.

Il avait oublié l'Afrique.

Mais quand on s'aperçut qu'une race (d'hommes?)

Devait encore à Dieu son tribut de sang noir, on lui fit un rappel.

Elle solda.

Et solde encore, et lorsqu'elle demanda sa place au sein de l'oecumène, on lui désigna quelques bancs. Elle s'assit. Et s'endormit.

Jésus étendit les mains sur ces têtes frisées, et les nègres furent sauvés.

Pas ici-bas, bien sûr.

Mais le royaume du ciel aux simples étant ouvert, ils y entrèrent en foule, et la Parole rapporte que, pour achever le miracle et laver pour toujours les noirs de l'originel péché, ils sont là-haut transformés en blancs, pour quoi l'on ne voit pas (sauf dans les films américains) d'anges ni de saints noirs.

Et c'est depuis ce temps que, semblable aux orties, la race nègre encombre les moissons d'âmes.

Et pousse ses surgeons partout où quelque faux s'apprête à séparer la vie de la terre étrangère

Partout

où des pêcheurs doivent être sauvés et des grâces rendues

God, one day having come down to earth, was saddened by the attitude of his creatures toward creation. He ordered the flood, and planted, on the resurgent land, a seed of need.

The ark, people, the world, and slowly, slowly, humanity arose from the ages without light to the ages without rest.

He had forgotten Africa.

Christ redeemed the evil man and built His church at Rome. His voice was heard in the desert. The Church over Society, Society over the Church, one carrying the other, founded civilization, in which man, docile to ancient wisdom, in order to appease the old gods not dead, slaughtered every ten years several millions of victims.

He had forgotten Africa.

But when one noticed that a race (of men?)

Still owed to God its tribute of black blood, they appealed to Him.

It bargained.

And still bargains, and when it asked for its seat in the bosom of ecumenicity, it was shown a few benches. It sat down. And it fell asleep.

Jesus extended his hands over those curly heads, and Negroes were saved.

Not here-below, of course.

But the Kingdom of Heaven being opened to the simple, they entered there in crowds, and the Word recounts that, in order to fulfill the miracle and wash blacks forever of the original sin, they were transformed up there into whites, which explains why one does not see (except in American movies) either black saints or black angels.

And it has been since that time that, like nettles, the Negro race encumbers the harvest of souls,

And sprouts offshoot wherever some scythe makes ready to separate life from hostile [foreign] land.

Everywhere
Where sinners must be saved and pardons given. Every-

Partout
où le sang de l'homme doit racheter les faiblesses de la
chair de l'homme
Partout où il faut peiner
Partout bêcher
Partout où la sueur et le sang ont fondé les sept piliers
Là où l'on meurt
Là où l'on tue
Danse, comme un feu follet aux flancs d'un morne vert
Là où il faut que soient pour le rythme du monde des
bottes cirées et des ascenseurs proférés
Comme une prière au ciel.

Et Dieu dit: "C'est bien!

Car pour être une race de feignants, ça, c'est une race
de feignants.
Je leur en foutrai, moi, la paix nazaréenne
Jusqu'à ce qu'ils en crèvent.
Et je leur en mettrai, moi, des croix dans le derrière,
des blanches
des rouges
des bleues et des trois couleurs ensemble pour n'en
pas oublier
des en pierre
des en bois
des romaines, des gammées, des lorraines jusqu'à ce
qu'ils en voient des étoiles.

Et les ferai monter par des sentiers arides jusqu'à la
porte étroite
Et les laisserai dehors pour qu'ils blanchissent au soleil
Et ceux qui ne seront pas dignes d'être élus, je m'en
vais les commettre à Mahomet."
Et Balthazar
Et Melchior dirent: "C'est bien, que votre volonté
soit faite et non la nôtre et pour l'éternité."

Et voici: Mélanie, la vieille bonne, tous les matins
que Dieu fait, s'en va, clopinant, porter son petit cierge
sur l'autel de ses péchés rédimés, prier pour le salut de
l'âme de ses frères inconscients, et que règne la paix sur
la terre des hommes.

Mais, moi, je n'aime pas cette Afrique-là.

where, where the blood of man must redeem the weaknesses of man's flesh. Everywhere, where one must slave and dig; where sweat and blood have founded the seven pillars; where one dies; where one kills, dances, like a will-o-the-wisp on the flanks of a green hillock; where, for the rhythm of the world, boots must be shined and elevators uplifted

Like a prayer to Heaven.

And God said: "It is good. For, to be a race of pretenders, *they* are a race of pretenders.

Me, I spit on their Nazarean tripe

Until they die of it.

And I'll stick some crosses up their behinds,

some white ones

some red ones

some blue and some three-colored ones so as not to forget any

some stone ones

some wooden ones

some Roman ones, some swastika-shaped ones, some Lorraine ones until they see stars from it.

And I'll make them climb by arid paths up to the strait and narrow gate. And I'll leave them outside so they'll whiten in the sun.

And those who shall not be worthy of being chosen, I shall commit to Mohammed."

And Balthazar.

And Melchior said: "That's good. May your will be done and not ours for all eternity."

And here: Melanie, the old servant, every morning that God makes, goes away, hobbling, carrying her little candle to the altar of her redeemed sins, to pray for the soul of her unconscious brothers, and that there may be peace on the earth of men.

But, me, I do not like that Africa.

L'Afrique des scorpions blancs mordant leur queue de sable
L'Afrique de la brousse étalée en une house épithéliale
L'Afrique à la terre ocre du sang des martyrs délavés
L'Afrique de la barre ceinte ainsi qu'un pendu qui fermente
Pour punir le crime de viol de la corde et des fagots
L'Afrique recroquevillée en souffrances non feintes
L'Afrique des plaines où poussent les seuls obis de mon enfance
L'Afrique des cactées boxant les baobabs rasés de près
L'Afrique des deux justices et d'un seul crime.

Non, je n'aime pas cette Afrique-là.

Et c'est à moi maintenant d'interroger:
Que répondras-tu à ton Dieu au jour du Jugement
Quand il te demandera: "Qu'as-tu fait de mon peuple?
J'ai confié des hommes à des hommes pour leur enseigner l'amour, et voici que l'écume de haine a mordu comme acide sur la terre.
As-tu fait paître mon troupeau l'herbe dure des sommets?
J'ai voulu une terre où les hommes soient hommes
et non loups
et non brebis
et non serpents
et non caméléons.
J'ai voulu une terre où la terre soit nourricière où la semence soit semence
où la moisson soit faite avec la faux de l'âme
une terre de Rédemption et non de Pénitence
un sol de tiges vertes et de troncs droits où l'homme porte sans faiblir la gravité des étoiles.
Es-tu digne de laver les pieds nus de mon peuple?

Responds."

Que lui répondras-tu, et lui répondras-tu? . . .

L'Afrique va parler.

Car c'est à elle maintenant d'exiger:
"J'ai voulu une terre où les hommes soient hommes
et non loups
et non brebis

The Africa of white scorpions biting their sand-colored tails,

The Africa of the bush spread out in an epithelial swell,

The Africa of the ochre earth, the color of the blood of diluted martyrs.

The Africa of the girded bar, similar to a hanged man who ferments,

To punish the crime of rape, rope, and faggots.

The Africa dried up in non-feigned suffering

The Africa of plains where grow the only sashes [ornaments] of my childhood

The Africa of cactus boxing close-cropped baobabs

The Africa of two justices and one crime.

I do not like that Africa.

And now it's my turn to ask questions:

What will you answer God on Judgment Day?

When He shall ask you: "What hast thou done with my people?

I entrusted men to men to be taught love, and lo and behold! The ecumenicity of hatred has bitten like an acid on earth.

Hast thou led my sheep to graze on the hard grass of the summits?

I wanted a land where men are men, and

not wolves

not sheep

not serpents

not chameleons.

I wanted an earth where the land is nurturing, where the seed is seed.

Where the harvest is made with the scythe of the soul, a land of Redemption and not Penitence.

A land of green buds and upright trunks where man bears, without weakening, the gravity of the stars.

Art thou worthy to wash the bare feet of my people? Answer!"

What will you answer Him?

Africa is going to speak

For it is her turn now to demand:

"I wanted a land where men are men

and not wolves

and not sheep

et non serpents
et non caméléons.

J'ai voulu une terre où la terre soit terre
Où la semence soit semence
Où la moisson soit faite avec la faux de l'âme, une terre de Rédemption et non de Pénitence, une terre d'Afrique.
Des siècles de souffrance ont aiguisé ma langue
J'ai appris à compter en gouttes de mon sang, et je reprends les dits des généreux prophètes
Je veux que sur mon sol de tiges vertes l'homme droit porte enfin la gravité du ciel."

Et ne lui réponds pas, il n'en est plus besoin, écoute ce pays en verve supplétoire, contemple tout ce peuple en marche promissoire, l'Afrique se dressant à la face des hommes sans haine, sans reproches, qui ne réclame plus mais affirme.
Il est encore des bancs dans l'Église de Dieu
Il est des pages blanches aux livres des Prophètes.
Aimes-tu l'aventure, ami? Alors regarde
Un continent s'émeut, une race s'éveille
Un murmure d'esprit fait frissonner les feuilles
Tout un rythme nouveau va térébrer le monde
Une teinte inédite pleuplera l'arc-en-ciel
Une tête dressée va provoquer la foudre.

L'Afrique va parler.

L'Afrique d'une seule justice et d'un seul crime
Le crime contre Dieu, le crime contre les hommes
Le crime de lèse-Afrique
Le crime contre ceux qui portent quelque chose.

Quoi?

un rythme
une onde dans la nuit à travers les forêts, rien — ou une âme nouvelle
un timbre
une intonation
une vigueur
un dilatement

and not serpents
and not chameleons.
I wanted a land where the land is land
Where seed is seed
Where the harvest is done with the scythe of the soul,
a land of Redemption and not of Penitence, a land of
Africa.
Centuries of suffering have sharpened my tongue;
I have learned to count in the drops of my blood, and
I am taking over the sayings of the generous Prophets
I wish that on my soil of green buds upright man
wear, finally, the gravity of heaven."

And do not answer him; there's no longer need to,
listen to this country in suppletory verve, contemplate
all this people in promissory march, Africa rising up
facing men without hate, without reproach, which no
longer demands but affirms.
There are still benches in God's church;
There are white pages in the books of the Prophets.

Do you like adventure, friend? Then look:
A continent bestirs itself, a race awakens.
A murmur of the mind makes the leaves rustle.
A whole new rhythm is going to burrow into the
world.
An unpublished hue will people the rainbow.
A reared head is going to provoke thunder

Africa is going to speak.

The Africa of one single justice and one single crime.
Crime against God, crime against men,
Crime against Africa,
Crime against those who carry something.

What?

a rhythm
a wave in the night through forests — or a new soul
a timbre
an intonation
a vigor
a dilation

une vibration qui par degrés dans la moelle déflue, révulse dans sa marche un vieux coeur endormi, lui prend la taille et vrille

et tourne

et vibre encore, dans les mains, dans les reins, le sexe, les cuisses et le vagin, descend plus bas

fait claquer les genoux, l'article des chevilles, l'adhérence des pieds, ah! cette frénésie qui me suinte du ciel.

Mais aussi, ô ami, une fierté nouvelle qui désigne à nos yeux le peuple du désert, un courage sans prix, une âme sans demande, un geste sans secousse dans une chair sans fatigue. . . .

a vibration which by degrees flows in the mallow, reawakens, in its march, a sleeping heart; takes its measure, and drills and turns,

and vibrates still, in the hands, in the back, the sex, the thighs and the vagina, goes down

lower still and makes the knees clank, the article of the ankles, the adherence of the feet, ah! that new frenzy which trickles down from heaven.

But, also, O friend, a new pride which points out to our eyes the people of the desert, priceless courage, a soul without demand, a gesture without shudder in the flesh without fatigue. . . .

Jean-F. Brière

Another product of Haiti, the only black republic in the Western Hemisphere, is Jean-F. Brière, who was born on November 28, 1909, at Jérémie. Educated in his native island, he served his country as a teacher, as supervisor of schools, and as *Chargé des Affaires Culturelles* in the Department of Foreign Affairs *(Affaires Extérieures)*.

Like his compatriot, Jacques Roumain, Brière was early a part of the revolutionary action of which his cultural activism was but one aspect. He founded the opposition newspaper, *La Bataille* [The Battle], and as a result of his attacks on the government he was imprisoned several times, spending fifteen months behind bars the last time because of his involvement in the case of *"Cri des Nègres"* ["the Negroes' Cry"], which occasioned a political controversy.

Brière's work bears the stamp of militancy. His language is simple and direct, a style bordering on prose. But his outpouring of words, "that river of words," as Senghor says of his poems in *Anthologie de la nouvelle poési nègre et Malgache,* "often transports great images swollen with suffering like cadavers of unburied heroes." [4]

Brière's *"Me revoici, Harlem,"* which is an expression of color solidarity among blacks, follows:

Me revoici, Harlem [5]

Au souvenir des lynchés de Géorgie
victimes du fascisme blanc.

Frère Noir, me voici ni moins pauvre que toi,
Ni moins triste ou plus grand. Je suis parmi la foule
L'anonyme passant qui grossit le convoi,
La goutte noire solidaire de tes houles.

Vois, tes mains ne sont pas moins noires que nos mains,
Et nos pas à travers des siècles de misère
Marquent le même glas sur le même chemin:
Nos ombres s'enlaçaient aux marches des calvaires.

Car nous avons déjà côte à côte lutté.

---

[4] Senghor, *op. cit.,* p. 121.
[5] Jean F. Brière, "Me revoici, Harlem," as quoted in Senghor, *op. cit.,* pp. 122-123.

Here I Am Again, Harlem

To the memory of those lynched in
Georgia, victims of white fascism

Black Brother, here I am again neither less poor than you,
Nor less sad or greater. I am among the crowd
The anonymous passerby who swells the procession,
The jointly responsible black drop of your surge.

See, your hands are not less black than my hands,
And our steps through the centuries of misery
Striking the same knell on the same road:
Our shadows are intertwined on the steps of the stations
   of the Cross.

For we have already fought side by side,

Lorsque je trébuchais, tu ramassais mes armes,
Et de tout ton grand corps par le labeur sculpté,
Tu protégeais ma chute et souriais en larmes.

De la jungle montait un silence profond
Que brisaient par moments d'indicibles souffrances.
Dans l'âcre odeur du sang je relevais le front
Et te voyais dressé sur l'horizon, immense.

Nous connûmes tous deux l'horreur des négriers . . .
Et souvent comme moi tu sens des courbatures
Se réveiller après les siècles meurtriers,
Et saigner dans ta chair les anciennes blessures.

Mais il fallut nous dire adieu vers seize cent.
Nous eûmes un regard où dansaient des mirages,
D'épiques visions de bataille et de sang:
Je revois ta silhouette aux ténèbres des âges.

Ta trace se perdit aux rives de l'Hudson.
L'été à Saint-Domingue accueillit mon angoisse,
Et l'écho me conta dans d'étranges chansons
Les Peaux-Rouges pensifs dont on défit la race.

Les siècles ont changé de chiffres dans le temps.
Saint-Domingue, brisant les chaînes, les lanières,
— L'incendie étalant sa toile de titan —
Arbora son drapeau sanglant dans la lumière.

Me revoici, Harlem. Ce Drapeau, c'est le tien,
Car le pacte d'orgueil, de gloire et de souffrance,
Nous l'avons contracté pour hier et demain:
Je déchire aujourd'hui les suaires du silence.

Ton carcan blesse encor mon cri le plus fécond.
Comme hier dans la cale aux sombres agonies,
Ton appel se déchire aux barreaux des prisons,
Et je respire mal lorsque tu t'asphyxies.

Nous avons désappris le dialecte africain,
Tu chantes en anglais mon rêve et ma souffrance,
Au rythme de tes blues dansent mes vieux chagrins,
Et je dis ton angoisse en la langue de France.

Le mépris qu'on te jette est sur ma joue à moi.

When I stumbled, you picked up my arms,
And with all your tall body carved out by toil,
You prevented me from falling and smiled tearfully.

From the jungle a profound silence arose
Which broke momentarily unspeakable sufferings.
In the pungent odor of blood I raised my head
And saw you erect on the horizon, immense.

We both knew the horror of the slave-ship . . .
And often like me you feel the stiffness
Reawaken after murderous centuries,
And you feel old wounds bleed in your flesh.

But we had to take leave of each other around sixteen
    hundred.
We had a gaze where danced mirages,
Of epic visions of battle and blood!
I see again your silhouette in the darkness of the ages.

Your trace was lost on the banks of the Hudson.
Summer in Santo-Domingo greets my anguish,
And the echo tells me in strange songs
The sensitive Redskins whose race one undid [destroyed].

The centuries have changed numbers in time.
Santo-Domingo, breaking the chains, the thongs,
The fire spreading your gigantic canvas
Hoisted its bloody flag in the light.

Here I am again, Harlem. This flag is yours,
For the pact of pride, of glory and of suffering.
We contracted it for today and tomorrow:
I am tearing up today the shroud of silence.

Your iron collar still wounds my most fecund cry,
Like yesterday in the hold of slave ships with dark
    agonies,
Your call echoes through prison bars,
And I breathe with difficulty when you struggle for
    breath.

We have forgotten the African dialect,
You sing in English my dream and my suffering.
To the rhythm of your blues my old sorrows dance,
And I tell your anguish in the language of France.

The scorn aimed at you is on my own cheek.

Le Lynché de Floride a son ombre en mon âme,
Et du bûcher sanglant que protège la loi,
Vers ton coeur, vers mon coeur monte la même flamme.

Quand tu saignes, Harlem, s'empourpre mon mouchoir.
Quand tu souffres, ta plainte en mon chant se prolonge.
De la même ferveur et dans le même soir,
Frère Noir, nous faisons tous deux le même songe.

The Florida lynch victim has his shadow in my soul,
And from the bloody funeral-pyre protected by law,
Toward your heart, toward my heart the same flame rises.

When you bleed, Harlem, my handkerchief is tinged
with purple.
When you suffer, your lament is prolonged in my song.
With the same fervor in the same evening,
Black Brother, we two dreamed the same dream.

Black Soul [6]

(fragment)

Je vous ai recontré dans les ascenseurs
à Paris.
Vous vous disiez du Sénégal ou des Antilles.
Et les mers traversées écumaient à vos dents,
hantaient votre sourire,
chantaient dans votre voix comme au creux des rochers.
Dans le plein jour des Champs-Élysées
je croisais brusquement vos visages tragiques.
Vos masques attestaient des douleurs centenaires.
A la Boule-Blanche
ou sous les couleurs de Montmartre,
votre voix,
votre souffle,
tout votre être suintait la joie.
Vous étiez la musique et vous étiez la danse,
mais persistait aux commissures de vos lèvres,
se déployait aux contorsions de votre corps
le serpent noir de la douleur.

A bord des paquebots nous nous sommes parlé.
Vous connaissiez les maisons closes du monde entier,
saviez faire l'amour dans toutes les langues.
Toutes les races avaient pâmé
dans la puissance de vos étreintes.
Et vous ne refusiez la cocaïne ni l'opium
que pour essayer d'endormir
au fond de votre chair la trace des lanières,
le geste humilié qui brise le genou
et, dans votre coeur,
le vertige de la souffrance sans paroles.
Vous sortiez de la cuisine
et jetiez un grand rire à la mer
comme une offrande perlée.
Mais quand le paquebot vibrait
de rires opulents et de joies luxueuses,
l'épaule lourde encor du faix de la journée,
vous chantiez pour vous seul, dans un coin de l'arrière,
vous aidant de la plainte amère du banjo,
la musique de la solitude et de l'amour.
Vous bâtissiez des oasis

[6] Jean-F Brière, "Black Soul," as quoted in Senghor, *op. cit.,*
pp. 124-128.

100

Black Soul
(fragment)

I have met you in the elevators of Paris.
You said you were from Senegal or the West Indies.
And the seas you crossed foamed in your teeth,
haunted your smile,
sang in your voice as in the hollow of rocks.
In the full light of the Champs-Elysées
I suddenly encountered your tragic visages.
Your masks attested to centuries-old griefs.
At the Boule-Blanche [a Paris nightclub heavily fre-
    quented by blacks]
Or under the colors of Montmartre,
your voice,
your breath,
your whole being exuded joy.
You were music and you were dance,
but there persisted on the commissure of your lips,
there unfurled to the contortions of your body
the black snake of suffering.

On board steamers we spoke to each other.
You knew the closed houses the world over,
knew how to make love in all languages.
All races had swooned
in the power of your embrace.
And you refused neither cocaine nor opium
except to put to sleep,
in the depths of your flesh, the trace of the thong,
the humiliated gesture which breaks the knee
and, in your heart,
the dizziness of suffering without words.
You would come out of the kitchen
and would cast a great burst of laughter at the sea
like a pearly offering.
But when the boat would vibrate
with rich laughter and luxurious joys,
Your shoulder still heavy with the burden of the day,
You would sing for yourself alone, in a
corner of the stern,
Accompanying yourself with the bitter moan of the banjo,
the music of solitude and of love.
You would build oases

dans la fumée d'un mégot sale
dont le goût a celui de la terre à Cuba.
Vous montriez sa route dans la nuit
à quelque mouette transie
égarée dans l'épais brouillard
et écoutiez, les yeux mouillés,
son dernier adieu triste
sur le quai des ténèbres.

Tantôt vous vous dressiez, dieu de bronze à la proue
des poussières de lune aux diamants des yeux,
et votre rêve atterrissait dans les étoiles.

Cinq siècles vous ont vu les armes à la main
et vous avez appris aux races exploitantes
la passion de la liberté.
A Saint-Domingue
vous jalonniez de suicidés
et paviez de pierres anonymes
le sentier tortueux qui s'ouvrit un matin
sur la voie triomphale de l'indépendance.
Et vous avez tenu sur les fonts baptismaux,
étreignant d'une main la torche de Vertières
et de l'autre brisant les fers de l'esclavage,
la naissance à la Liberté
de toute l'Amérique Espagnole.
Vous avez construit Chicago
en chantant des blues,
bâti les États-Unis
au rythme des spirituals
et votre sang fermente
dans les rouges sillons du drapeau étoilé.
Sortant des ténèbres,
vous sautez sur le ring:
champion du monde,
et frappez à chaque victoire
le gong sonore des revendications de la race.
Au Congo,
en Guinée,
vous vous êtes dressé contre l'impérialisme
et l'avez combattu
avec des tambours,
des airs étranges
où grondait, houle omniprésente,
le choeur de vos haines séculaires.

on the smoke of a dirty cigarette butt
which tasted like the earth in Cuba.
You would show the way in the night
to some benumbed deaf-mute
lost in the thick fog;
and you would listen, with moist eyes,
to his last sad good-bye
on the wharf of darkness.

Sometimes you rose up, a bronze god on the prow
of the dust of the moon to the diamond of the eyes,
and your dream landed in the stars.

Five centuries have seen you with your arms in hand,
and you have taught the exploiting races
the passion of freedom.
In Santo-Domingo
You staked out with suicides
and paved with anonymous stones
the tortuous path which opened one morning
on the triumphal road to independence.
And you held on the baptismal fonts,
pressing in one hand the torch of Vertières
and in the other breaking the shackles of slavery,
the birth of the Liberty
of all Spanish America.
You constructed Chicago
while singing the blues,
built the United States
to the rhythm of the spirituals,
and your blood ferments
in the red furrows of the star-spangled banner.
Coming out of the darkness,
you jump into the ring:
Champion of the world,
and you strike, at each victory,
the gong of the demands of the race.
In the Congo,
in Guinea,
you rose up against imperialism
and you fought it
with drums,
with strange airs
where groaned, in an omnipresent swell,
the chorus of your centuries-old hatreds.

Vous avez éclairé le monde
à la lumière de vos incendies.
Et aux jours sombres de l'Éthiopie martyre,
vous êtes accouru de tous les coins du monde,
mâchant les mêmes airs amers,
la même rage,
les mêmes cris.
En France,
en Belgique,
en Italie,
en Grèce,
vous avez affronté les dangers et la mort . . .
Et au jour du triomphe,
après que des soldats
vous eussent chassé avec René Maran
d'un café de Paris
vous êtes revenu
sur des bateaux
où l'on vous mesurait déjà la place
et refoulait à la cuisine,
vers vos outils,
votre balai,
votre amertume,
à Paris,
à New-York,
à Alger,
au Texas,
derrière les barbelés féroces
de la Mason Dixon Line
de tous les pays du monde.
On vous a désarmé partout.
Mais peut-on désarmer le coeur d'un homme noir?
Si vous avez remis l'uniforme de guerre,
vous avez bien gardé vos nombreuses blessures
dont les lèvres fermées vous parlent à voix basse.

Vous attendez le prochain appel,
l'inévitable mobilisation,
car votre guerre à vous n'a connu que des trêves,
car il n'est pas de terre où n'ait coulé ton sang,
de langue où ta couleur n'ait été insultée.
Vous souriez, Black Boy,
vous chantez,
vous dansez,

You lighted up the world
by the glow of your fires.
And during the dark days of martyred Ethiopia,
you came forth from all corners of the world,
chanting the same bitter tunes,
the same rage,
the same cries.
In France,
in Belgium,
in Italy,
in Greece,
you faced dangers and death . . .
And on the day of triumph,
after soldiers
had driven you with René Maran
from a Paris café
you came back on boats
on which they were already meting out your place
and relegating you to the kitchen,
toward your utensils,
your broom,
your bitterness;
in Paris,
in New York,
in Algiers,
in Texas,
behind the ferocious barbed-wire
of the Mason-Dixon Line
of all countries of the world.
They disarmed you everywhere.
But can one disarm the heart of a black man?
If you have put away the uniform of war,
you have kept well your numerous wounds,
whose closed lips speak to you in whispers.

You await the next call,
the inevitable mobilization,
for your own war has known only truces,
for there is no land where your blood has not flowed,
no language in which your color has not been insulted.
You smile, Black Boy,
you sing,
you dance,

vous bercez les générations
qui montent à toutes les heures
sur les fronts du travail et de la peine,
qui monterez demain à l'assaut des bastilles
vers les bastions de l'avenir
pour écrire dans toutes les langues,
aux pages claires de tous les ciels,
la déclaration de tes droits méconnus
depuis plus de cinq siècles,
en Guinée,
au Maroc,
au Congo,
partout enfin où vos mains noires
ont laissé aux murs de la Civilisation
des empreintes d'amour, de grâce et de lumière. . . .

you lull the generations
which mount at all hours
on the fronts of work and of toil,
which will mount tomorrow the assault on the bastilles
toward the bastions of the future
in order to write in all languages,
on the clear pages of all skies,
the declarations of thy rights unrecognized
for more than five centuries,
in Guinea,
in Morocco,
in the Congo,
everywhere, finally, where your black hands
have left on the walls of civilization
imprints of love, grace and light. . . .

David Diop

David Diop was born in Bordeaux, France, of a Senegalese mother and a Camerounese father. Some of his childhood was spent in each of the following places: Cameroun, Senegal, and France. Early in his life he started writing poetry which was published in *Présence Africaine.*

Two of his early poems follow:

Un Blanc m'a dit. . . .[7]

Tu n'es qu'un nègre!
Un nègre!
Un sale nègre!
Ton coeur est une éponge qui boit
Qui boit avec frénésie le liquide empoisonné du Vice
Et ta couleur emprisonne ton sang
Dans l'éternité de l'esclavage.
Le fer rouge de la justice t'a marqué
Marqué dans ta chair de luxure.
Ta route a les contours tortueux de l'humiliation
Et ton avenir, monstre damné, c'est ton présent de honte.
Donne-moi ce dos qui ruisselle
Et ruisselle de la sueur fétide de tes fautes.
Donne-moi tes mains calleuses et lourdes
Ces mains de rachat sans espoir.
Le travail n'attend pas!
Et que tombe ma pitié
Devant l'horreur de ton spectacle.

[7] David Diop, "Un Blanc m'a dit . . .," *Présence Africaine,* as quoted in Senghor, *op. cit.,* p. 175.

A White Man Said to Me. . . .

You are nothing but a nigger!
A nigger!
A damn nigger!
Your heart is a sponge which drinks,
Which drinks frantically the poisoned liquid of Vice
And your color imprisons your blood
In the eternity of slavery.
The red iron of justice has marked you,
Marked you in your lewd flesh.
Your route has the tortuous contours of humiliation
And your future, accursed monster, is your shameful
    present
Give me that dripping back,
Dripping with the stinking sweat of your errors.
Give me your callous, heavy hands,
Those hands of hopeless redemption.
Work awaits not!
And may my pity fall
Before the horrible sight of you.

Souffre, pauvre Nègre [8]

Souffre, pauvre Nègre! . . .
Le fouet siffle
Siffle sur ton dos de sueur et de sang
Souffre, pauvre Nègre!
Le jour est long
Si long à porter l'ivoire blanc du Blanc ton Maître
Souffre, pauvre Nègre!
Tes enfants ont faim
Faim et ta case est vide
Vide de ta femme qui dort
Qui dort sur la couche seigneuriale
Souffre, pauvre Nègre!
Nègre noir comme la Misère!

[8] Diop, "Souffre pauvre Nègre," *Présence Africaine,* as quoted in Senghor, *op. cit.,* pp. 175-176.

Suffer, Poor Negro

Suffer, poor Negro! —
The whip hisses,
Whistles on your sweaty, bloody back.
Suffer, poor Negro!
The day is long,
So long to carry the white ivory of your White Master.
Suffer, poor Negro!
Your children are hungry,
Hungry, and your cabin is empty,
Empty of your wife who is sleeping
Sleeping on the Master's couch.
Suffer, poor Negro!
Negro black as Wretchedness.

Jacques Roumain

The preeminent Haitian poet is Jacques Roumain, who was also an outstanding novelist. His best-known novel is *Gouverneur de la Rosée*, which was translated into English under the title *Masters of the Dew* by Mercer Cook.

Roumain was born in the Haitian capital, Port-au-Prince, in 1907; he died in 1944. He traveled and spent some time in Switzerland, England, and Spain, as well as in France; he learned the language of each of these countries. Like Césaire and Senghor, he combined politics and poetry. The following poem of his is dedicated to Tristan Remy:

Nouveau sermon nègre [9]

Ils ont craché à Sa Face leur mépris glacé
Comme un drapeau noir flotte au vent battu par la neige
Pour faire de lui le pauvre nègre le dieu des puissants
De ses haillons des ornements d'autel
De son doux chant de misère
De sa plainte tremblante de banjo
Le tumulte orgueilleux de l'orgue
De ses bras qui halaient les lourds chalands
Sur le fleuve Jourdain
L'arme de ceux qui frappent par l'épée
De son corps épuisé comme le nôtre dans les plantations
    de coton
Tel un charbon ardent
Tel un charbon ardent dans un buisson de roses blanches
Le bouclier d'or de leur fortune
Ils ont blanchi Sa Face noire sous le crachat de leur
    mépris glacé

Ils ont craché sur Ta Face noire
Seigneur, notre ami, notre camarade
Toi qui écartas du visage de la prostituée
Comme un rideau de roseaux ses longs cheveux sur la
    source de ses larmes

Ils ont fait
    les riches les pharisiens les propriétaires fonciers les
    banquiers
Ils ont fait de l'homme saignant le dieu sanglant

[9] Jacques Roumain, "Nouveau sermon nègre," as quoted in Senghor, *op. cit.*, pp. 119-120.

New Negro Sermon

They spat in His Face their cold scorn
Like a black flag floating in the snow-beaten wind
To make of him the poor Negro the god of the powerful,
Of his rags some altar ornaments,
Of his mellow song of misery,
Of the trembling moan of his banjo,
The proud peal of the organ;
Of his arms which hauled the heavy barges
on the river Jordan
The arm of those who strike with the sword;
Of his body like ours exhausted on the cotton plantations
Like a burning ember,
Like a burning ember in a bush of white roses,
The golden shield of their fortune.
They have whitened His black Face under the sputum
of their cold scorn.

They have spat on your black face
Lord, our friend, our comrade,
Thou who didst draw away from the face of the
prostitute,
Like a curtain of reeds, her long hair over the source
of her tears.

They have made
the rich the pharisees, the land-owner, the bankers.
They have made of bleeding man the bloody god.

Oh Judas ricane
Oh Judas ricane:
Christ entre deux voleurs comme une flamme déchirée
   au sommet du monde
Allumait la révolte des esclaves
Mais Christ aujourd'hui est dans la maison des voleurs
Et ses bras déploient dans les cathédrales l'ombre étendue
   du vautour
Et dans les caves des monastères le prêtre compte les
   intérêts des trente deniers
Et les clochers des églises crachent la mort sur les multi-
   tudes affamées

Nous ne leur pardonnerons pas, car ils savent ce qu'ils
   font
Ils ont lynché John qui organisait le syndicat
Ils l'ont chassé comme un loup hagard avec des chiens
   à travers bois
Ils l'ont pendu en riant au tronc du vieux sycomore
Non, frères, camarades
Nous ne prierons plus
Notre révolte s'élève comme le cri de l'oiseau de tempête
   audessus du clapotement pourri des marécages
Nous ne chanterons plus les tristes spirituals désespérés
Un autre chant jaillit de nos gorges
Nous déployons nos rouges drapeaux
Tachés du sang de nos justes
Sous ce signe nous marcherons
Sous ce signe nous marchons
Debout les damnés de la terre
Debout les forçats de la faim.

Oh, Judas sneers,
Oh, Judas sneers!
Christ between two thieves like a torn flame at the top
of the world
Lighted the revolt of the slaves,
But Christ today is in the house of thieves,
And his arms unfold in the cathedrals the extended
shadow of the vulture
And in the cellars of the monasteries the priest counts
the interests of the thirty pieces of silver,
And the church bells spit death on the hungry
multitudes.

We will not forgive them, for they know what they do.
They lynched John, who was organizing the union;
They chased him with dogs, like a haggard wolf,
through the woods;
They hanged him, as they laughed, on the trunk of the
old sycamore.
No, brothers, comrades
We will pray no more.
Our revolt rises like the cry of the storm bird above
the rotten clicking of the swamps.
We will no longer sing the sad spirituals of despair.
Another song gushes from our throats.
We unfurl our red flags,
Stained with the blood of our just.
Under this sign we shall march;
Under this sign we are marching.
Stand up, ye wretched of the earth.
Stand up, ye convicts of hunger.

6
Conclusion

The poems included in this book reveal the scope and initial thrust of the *Négritude* school of writers who came to the attention of the French-reading public in the 1930's and 1940's. In the main, the writers in question were highly gifted and equipped with excellent intellectual training, and they include the creators and promulgators of the concept and the term *Négritude*.

It may be said that the common denominator of all these writers is consciousness of color and racial pride, complemented by a deep conviction of solidarity among all blacks, both in and outside Africa, who share a common heritage of oppression, injustice, poverty, and economic ills resulting therefrom. The reaction of the various proponents of *Négritude* to the whites responsible for their plight runs the gamut from Senghor's humane forgiveness to the indignation and bitterness of Césaire *et al.* Their poems are veritable laments amounting to variations on a common theme: the suffering, insults, and humiliations resulting from racist attitudes and practices the world over. They all came to accept Senghor's concept of *Négritude* as an arm of deliverance, a tool for the liberation of blacks from their present-day serfdom, for without belief in one's own potential and pride in one's own past and ancestral culture, as well as group solidarity, blacks would lack the basic essentials for launching any kind of social revolution or for initiating any kind of movement for liberation that could possibly succeed. It is doubtful that these early exponents of *Négritude* envisioned or thought of violent revolution as a possibility. Like the architects of the French Revolution, Montesquieu, Voltaire, and Rousseau, they sought social, economic, and political reforms within the system. The exception was Césaire, who, becoming progressively bitter and disillusioned, joined the Communist party.

The contact of Senghor, Césaire, and Damas with Paris, even in the early and middle 1930's, generated a center of African studies, long before the present vogue among Afro-Americans, which gave them a greater awareness of Africa and accentuated the marked differences between European and African civilizations. Moreover, in pitting the African's cultural heritage against the European's, they discovered numerous positive values in the former and many negative ones in the latter. Besides, they came to realize that there was nothing in their cultural past of which to be ashamed. They came gradually to reject, in part at least, the white man's concept of history and his belief in the superiority of European and Western cultures over what whites had traditionally labeled "primitive" societies. France had sought to make black Frenchmen of its African and West Indian Negroes, to assimilate them to French culture. While men like Césaire and Senghor blended with their French environment in language, intellect, education, dress, and manners and were fully accepted by white Frenchmen in the most elite circles, these men realized more and more that they were black and of African origin and that that fact alone made them different from their fellow whites. Assimilation could, therefore, never be complete even if they wanted to be assimilated, which ostensibly they did not.

Senghor, at least, approved limited assimilation, that is, adopting from European civilization that which could be of use in African cultures. "Assimilate but do not be assimilated" *("assimiler, non être assimilés")* is the objective of the Bard of Senegal, a sort of cultural grafting that combines the best of two worlds and lays the foundation for a stronger offshoot than either parent culture. Other *Négritude* poets reject Europe *in toto*. Damas is one of them. For example, he declares, "I have the impression of being ridiculous in their collar, their shoes. . . ."

Perhaps the most decisive factor in this birth of black consciousness was the hostility of whites, sometimes overt but most often subtly expressed toward them, a hostility that revealed itself through a stare, a slight, and at times through spoken insults. Not even "civilized" and "tolerant" Parisians were faultless in that regard. Such attitudes caused a rude awakening among alert black intellectuals who had imagined Paris to be free of racism. Senghor tells us:

> Put yourself in their skin, wake up one morning, black and colonized in the "shock of being seen" by the corrosive stare of the white man. They knew, those Negro students between the years of '25 and '35, that Europe, for three centuries, had taught to their fathers their nothingness—to the citizens of 1848. They had [according to Europeans] thought nothing, built nothing, painted nothing, sung nothing. They *were* nothing, at the bottom of the abyss, in the absoluteness of despair.[1]

Yet another factor in the birth of black awareness and solidarity among black expatriates in Paris in the decade 1925-1935 was their discovery of fellow black writers in the United States, such Afro-American literary pioneers of great talent as Alain Locke, an intellectual who interpreted to them the black experience in America and opened their eyes to the excellent writers of the Negro Renaissance, Charles W. Chesnutt, W. E. B. DuBois, Paul Lawrence Dunbar, Claude McKay, Countee Cullen, Langston Hughes, and Sterling A. Brown; novelists such as Jessie Fauset and Jean Toomer; painters Henry O. Tanner and William E. Scott; sculptors Meta Warrick Fuller, Mae Jackson, and Elizabeth Prophet. The meetings at Mlle. André Nardal's brought together blacks from two hemispheres and facilitated cross-fertilization of talent, unity of purpose, and color solidarity. Common ancestry and background, community in suffering, and long-pent-up resentments bridged the geographical distance separating these sons of Africa and endowed them with a *cause commune*. Indeed, the effect of Negro American intellectuals and writers on their African and West Indian counterparts was enormous. Senghor found in Countee Cullen a new vocabulary: "regal black," "strong bronzed men," "copper sun," etc. In James

[1] Translated from Léopold Sédar Senghor, "L'Apport de la poésie nègre du demi siècle," *Liberté* 1, p. 313.

Weldon Johnson and Langston Hughes, he delighted to the song of the black woman, black beauty (cf. *"Femme noire"*), and black land.

Africans and West Indians, like their Afro-American brothers, must have read with pride Langston Hughes' words.

> We younger artists who create now intend to express our individual darkskinned selves without fear or shame. If white people are pleased, we are glad. If they are not, it doesn't matter. . . . If colored people are pleased, we are glad. If they are not, their displeasure doesn't matter either.[2]

It is this literary outgrowth of a common black heritage that Senghor has in mind when he defines *Négritude* as "the sum-total of black values and the claiming of black civilizations" *(l'ensemble des valeurs noires et la revendication des civilsations noires").*[3]

It is not without significance that the creators and architects of the concept and term *Négritude* are masters of the French language who combine technical linguistic expertise, poetic sensitivity, and social commentary to construct an effective weapon in their fight for liberation, for human equality, and for universal brotherhood. The sole benefit of the ugly experience of European colonialism in Africa was, in our opinion, the fact of giving the former colonial subjects a *lingua franca,* French and English, depending on the colonizing country, with which to communicate with their fellow Africans across tribal lines and which was also a powerful vehicle for the dissemination of ideas and the achievement of independence, and, hopefully, eventual self-sufficiency and equality among the nations of the world.

This treatment of the writers of the *Négritude* school lays no claim to completeness. Other names from the French-speaking black countries of the world might have been included, and the scope of the book could have been extended to the present. We have limited this work, in time and space, so as to focus principally on the founders of the school since their works are the most exemplary manifestation of *Négritude*. We have, moreover, restricted the area covered by this study to one

[2] Langston Hughes, "The Twenties: Harlem and Its Négritude," *African Forum*, vol. 1, no. 4 (Spring, 1966), p. 19.

[3] Léopold Sédar Senghor, *Entretien de Juin,* as quoted in Lilyan Kesteloot, *Écrivains noirs de la langue française* (Brussels, Belgium: Institut de Sociologie, Université de Bruxelles, 1963), p. 110.

literary *genre* (style), poetry, a *genre* seldom associated with social commentary and protest. In so doing, we have not touched on the novel, the theater, and the essay, which have also been used with telling effect by some Afro-French writers. We have thus avoided discussing the works of the extremists and proponents of violent revolution as the only cure for the race problem. These latter find their archetype in the late Frantz Fanon, whose *Peau noire, Masques blancs* [Black Skin, White Masks] and *Les Damnés de la Terre* [The Wretched of the Earth] have become the bibles of the black extremists in the United States.

The purpose of this book has been to induct the reader into an understanding and appreciation of an excellent body of literary creativity placed in the service of black awareness, interracial tolerance, and racial liberation. An ancillary objective of the present opus is to show what mastery of a difficult communication medium blacks can achieve and how they can compete on equal footing with their former colonial masters, by proving that even in a second or adopted language "the pen is mightier than the sword."

Not all the poetry of the writers discussed in the present opus is protest-oriented. Much of the work is free of racial overtones and reflects such universal subjects as childhood reminiscences, ancestral worship, love of nature, and romance. By far the greater part of their poetic work, however, is inspired by the ever-present preoccupation with the problem of racial prejudice and its devastating effect on blacks. In these works, the poets herein treated sing in a minor key, but as the nineteenth century French Romantic poet, Alfred de Musset, reminds us:

Les plus désespérés sont les chants les plus beaux,
Et j'en sais d'immortels qui sont de purs sanglots.[4]

(The most despondent [i.e., the saddest] songs are the
most beautiful,
And I know some immortal ones that are pure sobs.)

[4] Alfred de Musset, "La Nuit de Mai," as quoted in Morris Bishop, *A Survey of French Literature* (New York: Harcourt Brace Jovanovich, Inc., 1955), p. 90.

Bibliography

Works of Léopold Sédar Senghor

Collections of Poems:

Chants d'ombre. Paris: Editions du Seuil, 1945.

Hosties Noires. Paris: Editions du Seuil, 1948.

Chants pour Naëtt. Paris: Editions Pierre Seghers, 1949.

Éthiopiques. Paris: Editions du Seuil, 1956.

Chants d'ombre et Hosties Noires. Paris: Editions du Seuil, 1956.

Nocturnes. Paris: Editions du Seuil, 1962.

Selected Poems. Translated and Introduced by John Reed and Clive Wake. New York: Atheneum Publishers, 1964.

Anthology:

Anthologie de la nouvelle póesie nègre et malgache de la langue française. Paris: Presses Universitaires de France, 1948 (new edition, 1969).

Collections of Essays and Prose Writings:

Liberté 1: Négritude et humanisme. Paris: Editions du Seuil, 1964.

Sur le socialisme Africain, first two essays first published in French in 1961 under the title *Nation et voie du socialisme,* and in 1962 in an English translation under the title of *Nationhood and the*

Road to African Socialism by Présence Africaine. Published in the U.S.A. under the title *On African Socialism*, translation by Mercer Cook. New York and London: Frederick A. Praeger, Inc., 1964.

Works of Aimé Césaire

Collections of Poems and Prose Works:

Les armes miraculeuses. Paris: Librairie Gallimard, 1946.

Cahier d'un retour au pays natal. Paris: Bordas, 1947, French-English edition, Paris: Présence Africaine, 1971.

Soleil cou coupé. Paris: Editions Fragrance, 1949.

Discours sur le colonialisme. Paris and Dakar: Présence Africaine, 1955.

Ferrements. Paris: Editions du Seuil, 1959.

Cadastre, including *Soleil cou coupé* and *Corps perdu.* Paris: Editions du Seuil, 1961.

Toussaint l'ouverture. Paris: Présence Africaine, 1962.

Plays:

Et les chiens se taisaient, theatrical version. Paris: Présence Africaine, 1956.

La Tragédie du roi Christophe. Paris: Présence Africaine, n.d.

Works of Léon-G. Damas

Pigments. Paris: Librairie J. Corti, 1939.
French edition, Paris: Présence Africaine, 1962.

Poètes noirs d'expression française. Paris: Editions du Seuil, 1947.

Graffiti. Paris: Pierre Seghers, 1952.

Black Label. Paris: Librairie Gallimard, 1956.

African Songs of Love, War, Grief, and Abuse. Ibadan, Nigeria: Mbari Publications, 1962.
Paperback edition, Evanston, Illinois: Northwestern University Press, 1963.

Related Works

Diop, David, *Coups de Pilon.* Paris: Présence Africaine, 1961.

Hughes, Langston, and Reygnault, Christine, editors, *Anthologie africaine et malgache.* Paris: Editions Pierre Seghers, 1962.

Kesteloot, Lilyan, *Aimé Césaire*. Paris: Editions Pierre Seghers, 1962.

_____, *Léopold Sédar Senghor*. Paris: Editions Pierre Seghers, 1961.

_____, *Les écrivains noirs de la langue française*. Brussels, Belgium: Institut de Sociologie, Université de Bruxelles, 1963.

Mezu, S. Okechukwu, *Léopold Sédar Senghor et la défense et illustration de la civilisation noire*. Paris: Librairie Marcel Didier, 1968.